A PROBLEM-FINDING APPROACH TO EFFECTIVE CORPORATE PLANNING

Recent Titles from Quorum Books

A Problem-Finding Approach to Effective Corporate Planning

ROBERT J. THIERAUF

Q QUORUM BOOKS
NEW YORK • WESTPORT, CONNECTICUT • LONDON

230782

658.401
T 435

1 0001 000 018 552

Library of Congress Cataloging-in-Publication Data

Thierauf, Robert J.
  A problem-finding approach to effective
corporate planning.

  Bibliography: p.
  Includes index.
  1. Corporate planning. 2. Problem solving.
I. Title.
HD30.28.T45 1987   658.4'012   87-5971
ISBN 0-89930-262-9 (lib. bdg. : alk. paper)

British Library Cataloguing in Publication Data is available.

Library of Congress Catalog Card Number: 87-5971
ISBN: 0-89930-262-9

First published in 1987 by Quorum Books

Greenwood Press, Inc.
88 Post Road West, Westport, Connecticut 06881

Printed in the United States of America

The paper used in this book complies with the
Permanent Paper Standard issued by the National
Information Standards Organization (Z39.48-1984).

10 9 8 7 6 5 4 3 2 1

"A danger foreseen is half avoided."

Thomas Fuller, M.D., 1732

Contents

Illustrations

Preface

For effective corporate planning in this ever-changing world, there is a great need to go beyond problem solving by focusing on problem finding. Today, corporate planners typically resort to solving short- to long-range problems facing an organization by using the traditional problem-solving process. In contrast, the latest thrust helpful in the realm of corporate planning is the problem-finding process. Basically problem finding looks out into the future and identifies those problems confronting the organization. In turn, these problems are brought back to the present time and solved so as not to jeopardize forthcoming organizational performance. In addition, problem finding identifies for implementation opportunities that are related to these future problems. Opportunities also can be identified by corporate planners for current operations.

The text looks at the underlying theory and practice of problem finding. To emphasize its practice and to illustrate the usefulness of this new approach, typical well-known corporations are presented. These examples are found in Chapters 1 through 9. Real-world examples are expanded in Chapters 10 through 12 to include the automobile, airline, and computer industries. This range of applications illustrates the viability of this broad approach for corporate planners.

In each chapter, there are a number of learning-oriented features. These include the following:

- *issues raised and explored* to stimulate the reader's interest;
- *outlines* of the important topical areas covered;
- *summaries* of the major topics discussed;
- *applications* of the problem-finding process to a wide range of business organizations.

Such an approach is helpful to the reader in bringing together the theory and practice of problem finding.

The structure of this book follows a logical sequence for presenting a comprehensive treatment of a problem-finding approach to effective corporate planning. Chapter 1 introduces the reader to the need for problem finding and its essentials. In Chapter 2, the detailed steps for the problem-centered and the opportunity-centered approach of the problem-finding process are set forth. Chapter 3 looks at management information systems, in particular, decision support systems as a means for implementing problem finding. Chapter 4 looks at the desired attributes of a corporate planner when engaged in problem finding. In Chapter 5 common difficulties experienced by a typical corporate planner are examined. Chapter 6 integrates corporate goals and critical success factors with problem finding. In Chapter 7 the essentials of strategic planning are related to the problem-finding process. In a similar manner, Chapters 8 and 9 examine tactical planning and operational planning, respectively, and their relationship to problem finding. Chapter 10 centers on the application of problem finding to the automobile industry. The same approach is used in Chapters 11 and 12 for the airline and computer industries, respectively. The bibliography focuses on past and current references to problem finding directly or indirectly.

In an undertaking of this type, I would like to thank the following professors at Xavier University for their insights and thoughts on the problem-finding process: Dr. Jerry Anderson, Dr. John Camealy, and Dr. Thomas Clark. In addition, it was a pleasure working with Mr. Thomas Gannon on this new direction in effective corporate planning.

PART I

RELATIONSHIP OF PROBLEM FINDING TO EFFECTIVE CORPORATE PLANNING

1

An Introduction to Problem Finding for Effective Corporate Planning

ISSUES RAISED AND EXPLORED

- What is the rationale for a new approach to corporate planning?
- What is the relationship of objectivity to problem finding in a typical business organization?
- What is the importance of the "management-by-perception" principle in the problem-finding process?
- How could problem finding have helped the Osborne Computer Corporation?

Newest Approach to Effective Corporate Planning Focuses on Problem Finding

   Utilization of Management-by-Perception Principle

   Problem-Centered and Opportunity-Centered Approaches

Current Approach to Corporate Planning Focuses on Problem Solving

   Utilization of Management-by-Exception Principle

   Quantitative-Centered and Decision-Centered Approaches

Corporate Planning Example Demonstrating the Need for Problem Finding: Osborne Computer Corporation

Summary

To set the stage for the entire text, this chapter looks initially at the rationale for problem finding in corporate planning. Additionally, reference is made to changing external and internal environmental factors. To make corporate planning more effective, there is a starting point, namely, the use of objectivity. This is followed by a discussion of a new management principle—"management by perception"—that is linked directly to the problem-finding process. In contrast, the "management-by-exception" principle is related to the current approaches to problem solving in resolving corporate planning problems. Finally, the chapter shows what happens when problem finding is ignored by management in the form of a real-world case study—the first of many to be presented in the text.

RATIONALE FOR A NEW APPROACH
TO CORPORATE PLANNING

In a dynamic and fast-changing world, there is a great need for timely and accurate business information for corporate planners. In the past, it generally has been undervalued, underestimated, and underused. But after personnel, it is a manager's most important resource.

A major problem facing today's corporate planners is the volume of information crossing their desks. It is so voluminous as to be almost unmanageable, yet good corporate planning of operations through effective decision making must be based on a steady flow of quality, up-to-date information. As John Naisbitt pointed out on the first page of his best-seller *Megatrends*, "Although we continue to think we live in an industrial society, we have in fact changed to an economy based on the creation and distribution of information." He calls this a *megashift*, an explosive transformation from an industrial to an information society. This shift is having an impact on all of us, particularly on the manner in which daily business is conducted. It necessitates the need to approach corporate planning from a new perspective. That is, corporate planning should center initially on problem finding; future information in the form of problems and related opportunities should be evaluated and resolved in the present as it affects the business organization tomorrow. This new way of thinking about corporate planning underlies the entire text.

Changing External Environmental Factors

Because the need for effective corporate planning information is of paramount concern to a typical business organization now and in the future, it is extremely important for the organization to coordinate its operations with the business universe. Of prime importance is information about markets in which the organization operates, current knowledge of its customers and competitors, availability of capital, capabilities of available personnel, and sources of supply. Increasing prices of purchased materials, rising labor costs, and foreign competition signal the need for some type of management information system (MIS) that describes the organization's economic environment and coordinates the external environment with the internal factors to provide corporate planning information.

Changing Internal Environmental Factors

The management information system, in addition to recognizing environmental trends external to the organization through problem finding, must treat changes that have occurred and that will occur in the internal business environment. Advancements in the behavioral sciences, continuing developments in management science, and increasing utilization of paperless computer output terminals must be reflected in the management information system. Interdepartmental approaches have transcended the traditional, functional lines of business in complex systems. Still other advances in development have been made regarding methods, procedures, computer equipment, and data communications equipment. By no means is this listing of internal factors complete, but it does serve to exemplify what is causing the organization's MIS to change to assist in corporate planning.

The changes taking place inside and outside the organization generally do not stand alone; each advancement tends to affect and overlap another. As a result, an effective management information system—that is, a decision support system (to be discussed in Chapter 3)—is capable of integrating these advances with the needs and capabilities of corporate planners. More frequent and more accurate information leads to better decisions, thereby leading to more effective corporate planning.

CHANGE OF THINKING IS NECESSARY TO MAKE CORPORATE PLANNING MORE EFFECTIVE

In light of the preceding comments concerning information, corporate planners of a typical business organization must rethink their ideas and views regarding the whole area of corporate planning. In the past, they have generally taken the very narrow viewpoint that there are problems to be solved (problem solving) which should be integrated into the corporate planning process. In effect, they are "coming in the back door." What corporate planners should be doing is "coming in the front door" by taking a different approach to their thinking. This means taking a much broader viewpoint of the entire organization than was taken in the past.

Need for Objectivity by Corporate Planners

In order for corporate planners to be as professional as possible in discharging their duties, the need for objectivity is paramount. Typically, the closer corporate planners get to a situation and the more directly they are involved and affected, the less objective they become. Few corporate planners would deny that the ability to remain objective is critical to the successful conduct of their jobs. Yet it is not a characteristic that a person either has or does not have. Rather, it is a characteristic that a person sometimes has and sometimes does not. The presence or absence of this element is usually related to how close the person is to a particular situation.

The potential for lack of objectivity has been recognized in many kinds of situations. Medical ethics limit physicians in treating members of their immediate family. In law, according to the adage, "A man who is his own lawyer has a fool for a client." Laws to define and restrict conflict-of-interest situations have become legion.

External Objectivity. The superior track records of corporate planners usually belong to those who have programmed their thinking processes so that they recognize when they are too close to a problem or decision. If and when it is appropriate, they do not hesitate to bring *external objectivity* to bear on the situation. Anyone can get to the point where he or she cannot see the forest for the trees, but not everyone can recognize this point. However, the effective corporate planner does.

Corporate planners are quick to recognize situations where they lack the specialized knowledge required to resolve a problem or decision. The obvious information void is not difficult to see although degrees of objectivity are much more difficult to define. The key to optimizing the organization's direction is the ability to recognize the point where internal objectivity is dangerously close to disappearing—the point where external sources of objectivity should be sought.

Approaches to Improve Objectivity for More Effective Corporate Planning

Dr. Leonard Sayles of Columbia University pointed out the need for, and effective use of, outside objectivity in an article in *Boardroom Reports.* "When making a critical decision . . . remember that . . . any group tends to become mesmerized as it talks up its convictions. Solution: Bring in an informed outsider who has not shared the group's experience and isn't fearful of being critical."[1] Thus, an approach to improving objectivity is the use of outside consultants.

Another approach to improve objectivity centers on making the latest thrust in management information systems or decision support systems available to corporate planners. This approach will be emphasized in future chapters.

Last, but not least, the use of a new structured approach to corporate planning is an effort to organize and improve objectivity. Such an approach emphasizes a problem-finding process that is complementary to the current problem-solving process. Essentially, this is the approach taken throughout the text. This new approach not only is capable of bringing together the external and internal environmental factors effectively but is capable of resolving the "trees versus the forest" syndrome that is typically found in corporate planning.

Overall, objectivity is a volatile commodity. It is not fixed; it can vary widely according to circumstances. It is related to corporate planners' closeness to the situation. Effective corporate planners know when they are too close, and they know what to do about it—use external consultants, decision support systems, and/or problem finding.

NEWEST APPROACH TO EFFECTIVE CORPORATE PLANNING FOCUSES ON PROBLEM FINDING

For a broad-based, objective viewpoint of corporate planning, two approaches to the problem-finding process are presented: the problem-centered approach and the opportunity-centered approach. Underlying the problem-finding process is the "management-by-perception" principle which is discussed first.

Utilization of Management-by-Perception Principle

The management-by-perception principle refers to the ability of management to perceive future external and internal trends before they occur and to determine their impact on new products and/or services so as to improve overall organizational performance.[2] It should be noted that this principle is forward looking as opposed to the backward-looking approach of management by exception, which focuses on comparison after the fact. However, in a typical company both have their place for decision making at the corporate planning level.

To elaborate further on management by perception, management must be able to perceive developing political and social trends that have relevance to the company. By perceiving these trends before they occur, management can adjust its strategic long-range plans for new products and/or services and, in turn, its tactical medium-range plans and operational short-range plans for them. In this manner, top management can improve overall performance for the company. In effect, they need to stand back and take a look at the total picture in which the company operates. Representative examples of a forward-looking approach that utilizes this principle include setting for an entire company strategic long-range plans and objectives that are fully integrated into the major systems and their related parts; planning and evaluating new products and/or services over their life cycles; acquiring short-, intermediate-, and long-term capital funds as needed for the entire company; and determining profit profiles on large alternative investment plans. These examples of a broad view generally make it easier for top management to accomplish desired company goals and objectives.

Problem-Centered and
Opportunity-Centered Approaches

For the *problem-centered approach*, logical-analytical thinking centers on examining the environment with the idea of looking into the future and exploring those problems that will have an impact on the company both now and at some time in the future. Essentially, problems identified in terms of the future (that is, problem finding) are brought back to the present time to examine their cause-and-effect relationships. The problem-centered approach includes dividing problems into their component parts, employing operational decision rules when deemed necessary, utilizing the language of numbers to quantify the parameters surrounding the problem, and searching for convergence, that is, for an answer.

Within the *opportunity-centered approach*, there is also need for logical-analytical thinking. However, the perspective is somewhat different in that the main focus is on identifying for the company opportunities to pursue that generally come from problems uncovered. In effect, the corporate planner needs to change an organizational liability into an asset, to identify problems that can result in important opportunities for the company.

From this enlightened view the opportunity-centered approach identifies important opportunities that are often overlooked by the problem-solving process which has been employed by the corporate planner. By taking off his or her "blinders," the corporate planner is able to look inside the problem and examine it thoroughly. Additionally, the opportunity-centered approach need not always be related to future problems. It can center on current opportunities that are identified by top management and/or the corporate planning staff. From this perspective, specific opportunities can be addressed directly by company members at the higher levels of management.

For the most part, these two approaches—problem centered and opportunity centered—are oriented toward semistructured and unstructured problems for a number of time periods—some short range and some medium to long range. Also, the problems found in problem finding require a thorough search not generally found with problem solving. Generally, the corporate planner finds a wide range of problems confronting him or her without looking too hard.

The specific steps of these two approaches to problem finding are different from each other. Nevertheless, their basic phases are the same. They are:

- *search*—looking for future problems and/or opportunities of concern to management;
- *identification*—specifying the problem or opportunity within its boundaries;
- *solution*—identifying the proper technique, method, and so on to solve the problem or pick the best opportunity;
- *implementation*—placing the solution into effect and monitoring the results.

The relationship of these basic phases of the problem-finding process will become apparent in the steps detailed in Chapter 2.

CURRENT APPROACH TO CORPORATE PLANNING FOCUSES ON PROBLEM SOLVING

Currently, the problem-solving process can be viewed as both a quantitative-centered approach and a decision-centered approach. Its underlying framework centers on the management-by-exception principle.

Utilization of Management-by-Exception Principle

The management-by-exception principle states that managers should concentrate their time and efforts on those areas that are in difficulty, leaving those areas that are doing unusually well alone. The control system should bring troubled areas to management's attention without obscuring them with massive quantities of useless data. Important elements for the effective use of this principle are (1) the prompt reporting of exceptions at critical control points, (2) the dissemination of information about these exceptions to those who have authority to take appropriate action, and (3) the initiation of corrective action when deemed necessary. The integration of these elements into the control system highlights an essential purpose of the system—detecting and correcting the deviations from predetermined plans and standards as operational activities progress.

Quantitative-Centered and Decision-Centered Approaches

The *quantitative-centered approach* is oriented toward solving well-structured problems for the short to medium range, and sometimes for the long range. The accent is on utilizing mathematical or statistical models (if deemed appropriate) that optimize performance (that is, maximize profits, minimize costs, or some other criterion) for one or more functional areas of a company. Essentially, the quantitative-centered approach is an extension of the scientific method (the scientific method was originally formulated by Francis Bacon in the sixteenth century and elaborated upon by John Stuart Mill in the nineteenth century) and employs a computerized approach to manipulate some type of quantitative model to solve the problem at hand.

In contrast, the accent for the *decision-centered approach* is on solving semistructured and unstructured problems for the short to medium range and sometimes for the long range. Additionally, the decision-centered approach encourages the integration of the manager's capabilities with that of a computerized mathematical or statistical model (if deemed appropriate), thereby increasing the quality of the final decision. A computerized interface with the corporate planner allows the individual to retain control throughout the entire problem-solving process. From this view, intuition, judgment, and experience are helpful in understanding how the environmental factors react to the stimuli that decisions provide. Of equal importance is a modeling approach that forces the corporate planner to evaluate the facts critically before reaching a final decision to the problem at hand. It should be noted that manual methods might be more appropriate for either approach to problem solving.

Although the detailed steps of the quantitative-centered and the decision-centered approaches to problem solving differ from one another, their basic phases are identical. They are:

- *identification*—specifying the real problem to be solved;
- *solution*—identifying the proper technique, method, and so on to solve the problem;
- *implementation*—placing the solution to the problem into effect and monitoring the results.

The tie-in of these basic phases of the problem-solving process and the detailed steps of each approach will be discussed in Chapter 2.

A comparison of the basic phases of problem finding to the basic phases of problem solving plus other differences is found in Figure 1.1. The real significance of these differences will be apparent in future chapters.

CORPORATE PLANNING EXAMPLE DEMONSTRATING THE NEED FOR PROBLEM FINDING: OSBORNE COMPUTER CORPORATION

The Osborne Computer Corporation founded in 1981 by Adam Osborne produced a portable computer, packed it with useful programs, and sold everything together for a low price. Its first machine was the Osborne 1, a twenty-six-pound machine that set off a computer revolution. The Osborne was a "wild success." In the machine's heyday, Osborne could not keep up with customer demand. Internally, however, there were few controls over operations. Employees were buying what they wanted, without management approval. Additionally, managers did not know how much inventory they had. Osborne did not have an efficient means of monitoring inventories of finished products. A computerized system that tracked manufacturing and order entry failed to work properly. Information management at the company was horrendous; problems were compounded by the company's rapid growth and a change of headquarters in December 1982.

As the corporation prospered and revenue climbed toward $100 million, Mr. Osborne realized that the corporation needed professional managers. He hired Mr. Robert Jaunich II, the

Figure 1.1
Comparison of problem finding to problem solving
from an overall standpoint

Basic Phases of the Problem-Finding Process—Accent on
Management by Perception:

Search   Identification   Solution   Implementation

Used to solve:

Semistructured Problems   Unstructured Problems

For the following time periods:

Some Short Range   Medium and Long Range

Basic Phases of the Problem-Solving Process—
Accent on Management by Exception:

Identification   Solution   Implementation

Used to solve:

Structured Problems Semistructured Problems Unstructured Problems

For the following time periods:

Short and Medium Range   Some Long Range

---

president of Consolidated Food Corporation, as its president. When Mr. Jaunich arrived, Osborne was preparing to go public. However, Jaunich received a surprise; namely, an audit uncovered a substantial loss. The corporation scrapped its public offering and sought private financing instead. It also clamped down on expenses. All expenditures, for example, had to be approved by a vice-president. However, the changes came too late since marketing miscalculations choked cash flow to a trickle in the spring of 1983.

More to the point, Osborne wanted to introduce a new product, the Executive portable computer, that was not supposed to be competitive with the original Osborne 1. But when dealers learned of the new machine in April, many canceled their orders for the Osborne 1. The Executive, however, was not ready for shipment until May and sales of Osbornes plummeted. There were periods when there was virtually no cash flow. By then, morale at Osborne Computer was poor. In essence, the camaraderie that is found in a new company when employees roll up their sleeves and work extra hard had gone.

Need for Problem Finding. With the introduction of the IBM Personal Computer (PC), Osborne's most significant mistake was failing to respond sooner to the dramatic changes in the computer market. From a corporate marketing viewpoint, problem finding was not employed; that is, management by perception was ignored in terms of new products coming on the market by the number-one computer manufacturer (IBM). The IBM PC became a "standard" almost overnight. Scores of computer companies now are producing IBM-compatible computers. Osborne did not realize how fast it had to move to change course. It was late in responding and suddenly the Osborne 1 was not selling anymore.

One computer developed by Osborne became obsolete before it was even introduced. The machine, code-named Vixen, was to be about ten pounds lighter than the original Osborne 1 and was originally set for introduction in December 1982. A poorly designed circuit board forced major delays in the Vixen product. Because cash had become tight at Osborne, the company's resources were moved from that project to the Executive II, the IBM-compatible machine. By the time Vixen was considered again, the IBM world had already passed it by. The corporation also feared the product might be eclipsed by new products due from IBM and Apple Computer, Inc. Thus, the Osborne Computer Corporation had lost its status as the only recognized producer of portables and was hard pressed to achieve similar prominence with any new machines. Osborne had three things going for it initially: price, bundled software, and portability. All those things were unique in the past. However, they are the lowest common demoninator in the market at this time and in the foreseeable future.

SUMMARY

The initial focus of the chapter was on the *megashift*—the shift from an industrial society to an information society. To make this transformation more orderly, the typical business organization needs to engage in problem finding to meet competition, if not beat it. A change of thinking is necessary before the problem-finding process is an integral part of the corporate planning process. Next, problem finidng was discussed as a way for corporate planners to achieve objectivity. The underlying framework for the problem-finding process was presented along with that for the traditional problem-solving process. In addition, the need for problem finidng was applied to the Osborne Computer Corporation. Overall, this chapter has set the stage for a full-scale treatment of the problem-finding process.

NOTES

1. Leonard Sayles, "Decision Making: Getting Other Opinions," *Boardroom Reports*, February 15, 1979, p. 5.

2. Robert J. Thierauf, Robert C. Klekamp, and Daniel W. Geeding, *Management Principles and Practices—A Contingency and Questionnaire Approach* (Santa Barbara, Calif.: Wiley/Hamilton, 1977), p. 773.

2

A Framework for the Problem-Finding Process

ISSUES RAISED AND EXPLORED

- What are the problem-finding techniques useful for corporate planners?
- What are the essentials of the quantitative-centered and the decision-centered approaches to problem solving?
- What are the detailed steps of the problem-centered and the opportunity-centered approaches to problem finding?
- What are typical corporate planning examples of the two approaches to the problem-finding process?

OUTLINE

The Problem-Finding Process and Effective Corporate Planning
Useful Problem-Finding Techniques for Corporate Planning
    Creative Thinking
    Brainstorming
    Synectics
    Problem Definition Table
    Checklists

This chapter builds upon Chapter 1 by examining and illustrating the detailed steps of the problem-centered and the opportunity-centered approaches to the problem-finding process. This comprehensive treatment of problem finding demonstrates that it complements problem solving such that both have their place within the corporate planning function. In other words, the entire range of problems confronted by corporate planners are encompassed by either the problem-finding process or the problem-solving process. Before discussing the methodology of problem finding, an introduction to it is given along with a presentation of useful problem-finding techniques. In addition, an overview of the problem-solving process is presented as a background for problem finding.

THE PROBLEM-FINDING PROCESS
AND EFFECTIVE CORPORATE PLANNING

In the current business literature, examples of approaches (quantitative or otherwise) to solve specific problems abound. Typically, one reads, "Consider the problem. . . ." But the really important questions are never asked, such as "How did the decision maker (that is, corporate planner) come to know this problem?" and "How does the decision maker (corporate planner) know that the problem is important enough to be solved?" Because the problem-solving process does not resolve these questions, there is need for a problem-finding process to address these important organizational questions and similar ones.

As in the problem-solving process, there is need in problem finding to go beyond relying on the accumulated experience of the corporate planner. In a similar manner, it is essential that the corporate planner go beyond focusing on analytical thinking. As noted in the previous chapter, it is necessary to go a step further by utilizing logical-analytical thinking. Logical-analytical thinking goes beyond analyzing present problems of a company as found in the problem-solving process. Its accent is on identifying future problems and their impact on the company today and tomorrow. Additionally, logical-analytical thinking is directed toward future problems that are actually opportunities in disguise. If the corporate planner has identified future problems, the individual has identified one or more opportunities. Based upon these views, the problem-finding process can be separated into a problem-centered approach and an opportunity-centered approach.

USEFUL PROBLEM-FINDING TECHNIQUES FOR CORPORATE PLANNING

A group of techniques that is broad in scope to assist in problem finding includes creative thinking, brainstorming, synectics, a problem definition table, and checklists. Due to its importance, each area will be discussed separately.

Creative Thinking

The main thrust of creative thinking in the problem-finding process is on new and untried approaches. The unusual approach and the exploration of generally nonstandard approaches and methods can often bring the corporate planner to the point where new alternatives can be devised for a problem under study. The period of incubation where new decision alternatives are fermenting finally results in the illumination stage. Too often, time for creative thinking is unduly restricted because there is the ever-pressing demand for immediate results. This is typically the fault of top management which does not recognize the importance of this creative phase in decision making at the levels below it.

Creativity requires a good logical mind that can reduce a complex situation to its essential elements. Effective corporate planners must think analytically and be highly imaginative in their approaches to decision making. Not only must they be able to visualize the possibilities of alternatives, they also must be capable of communicating their ideas in an understandable manner. They must take the initiative when required and answer valid objections to their work. In essence, they must operate effectively in two worlds—the *conceptual* one of creative problem finding and the *real* one of effective decisions.

During decision making, corporate planners who possess the above attributes should work with selected personnel from the various departments which can then act as a sounding board for new ideas and alternatives. Departmental representatives, who have the answers to the proverbial questions of who, what, where, when, how, and why, should be imaginative enough to recommend improvements to those set forth. Likewise, they should be objective in their thinking and should accept worthwhile changes. Facts that may be needed subsequently can be gathered under their direction. Corporate planners and departmental representatives can complement one another. This combination will produce better decisions than produced by corporate planners who work alone.

Brainstorming

Brainstorming, probably the best-known creativity technique, was developed by Alex F. Osborn to help solve advertising problems. It is used to improve problem analysis by providing more possible solutions and unusual approaches to the problem under study. A typical brainstorming group consists of six to twelve individuals who assemble to search for solutions to a problem. Most brainstorming experts recommend that the group members have a variety of backgrounds in order to facilitate the analysis of the problem from different points of view. Also, sessions lasting from forty minutes to one hour are most effective.

Osborn suggests four rules necessary for the utilization of brainstorming: (1) Judgment is withheld; ideas may be criticized and evaluated later. (2) Wild ideas are encouraged; ideas are easier to modify than to originate. (3) Numerous ideas are desired; more ideas increase the possibility of obtaining an excellent idea. (4) The participants are encouraged to utilize the ideas of others to develop additional ideas. Other recommended procedures include: the sessions should be recorded because some ideas may be missed during a meeting; the problem must be manageable, even if it requires breaking large problems into smaller parts; and samples should be available if products are being discussed.

Based upon the foregoing rules, the following guidelines should be observed to provide the proper environment for a brainstorming session:

- Do not attempt to generate new ideas and to judge them at the same time.
- Do try to generate a large quantity of possible solutions.
- Seek a wide variety of solutions by using different approaches to the problem.
- Listen carefully to the input of the others as an opportunity to "hitchhike" onto an idea or ideas, as a combination or improvement.
- During the session, no idea, even the most seemingly impractical, should be discarded.
- "Ridiculous" is an unheard-of word in brainstorming. It is both impolite and disastrous to the creative process.
- Before concluding the brainstorming exercise, some time should be allowed for *subconscious* thought about the problem while *consciously* discussing other possible solutions. This incubation can be extended to any appropriate time period—recycling and reorbiting as necessary.
- Recycling and backtracking are useful to a degree, but there should be an attempt to "lean" forward since this is where the solutions are to be found.

Once the session has adjourned, those whose problems were discussed will evaluate the ideas presented. Most of the ideas will be rejected based on common sense and logical judgment. In fact, it may turn out that none can be considered as potential solutions. However, the creative faculty of corporate planners and departmental representatives may provide the necessary impetus to modify one or more ideas as workable solutions to the problem under study. Thus, a specific problem area for implementation might not have the best solution if it were not for the brainstorming approach. A fresh look by an uninhibited and unrestricted free association can help solve problems where the proposed solutions are different from the existing ones.

Synectics

Synectics, which is not as well known as brainstorming, is based on the assumptions that creativity can be described and taught. Its purpose is to improve the quality of creative output from those assigned to a synectics team. The people selected to participate in a synectics group determine the group's success. For this reason, team members are chosen only after very thorough testing and screening in order to insure selection of the best combination needed to solve the problems of a specific organization. The selection process results in a tailor-made synectics team composed of individuals best equipped, intellectually and psychologically, to deal with problems unique to their organization. After selection, members are assigned to the synectics team and begin studying the creative process and learning the ways of synectics. A synectics team solves problems for the entire organization, similar to operations research (management science) or system analyst groups, and must be fully integrated into the organization.

Essentially, the synectic process involves two steps: (1) making the strange familiar and (2) making the familiar strange. The first step requires that the problem be understood and that the ramifications be considered. The mind tends to emphasize one's own experiences and to force strange ideas into an acceptable pattern. Thus, it is necessary to reorient these strange ideas into familiar ones. The second step, making the familiar strange, involves distorting, inverting, and transposing the problem in an attempt to view the problem from an unfamiliar perspective.

To assist in viewing the problem from different angles (making the familiar strange), synectics uses the following mechanisms:

- *personal analogy*—Members of the group try to identify, metaphorically, with elements of the problem. For example, when a synectics group attempted to develop a new constant-speed mechanism, each member of the group metaphorically entered the box and, using his or her body, tried to effect the speed consistency required. This eventually resulted in an efficient and economical model.

- *direct analogy*—Parallel facts are compared. Bell used direct analogy by studying the human ear when he invented the telephone. Biology is an excellent source for direct analogies.

- *symbolic analogy*—Objective and impersonal images are used to describe the problem. In one case, symbolic analogy was used in developing a jack to more heavy objects, such as houses or freight. The synectics group was making little progress until a member made a symbolic analogy with the Indian rope trick. This analogy proved to be the key and resulted in an innovative jacking mechanism.

- *fantasy analogy*—Fantasies are used to solve the problem. For example, a vapor-proof closure for a space suit was developed using a fantasy analogy of little insects closing the opening. This analogy led to the development of a complex spring mechanism for closure.

Problem Definition Table

Many problems arise for which no predetermined solution exists. Because corporate planners have difficulty in defining problems for which they have no immediate answer, it is exceedingly useful to perform a thorough job of defining problems and developing solutions later. It is sometimes just as important to state what the problem *is not* as it is to state what it *is* in order to identify and define it. Charles Kepner and Benjamin Tregoe have devised a helpful table (Table 2.1) for this purpose. By filling in the blank spaces in the table, the problem becomes more clearly defined and, as a result, closer to be solved.

Table 2.1
A problem definition table that relates "questions"
to what "is" and what "is not."

Questions	Is	Is Not
What?		
When?		
Who?		
Where?		
To What Extent?		

To complete this table, the corporate planner will ask the following questions about the problem and the overall situation:

- What is happening? What is not happening?
- When is it happening? When is it not happening?
- To whom is it happening? To whom is it not happening?
- Where is it happening? Where is it not happening?
- To what extent is it happening? To what extent is it not happening?

Within this framework, the corporate planner is prepared to define the problem more precisely prior to solving it.

Checklists

Another approach to problem finding is the use of checklists. Because problems can be broken down into sub-problems, which, in turn, can be solved by taking a series of identifiable steps, a checklist can be a particularly useful format in which to present these steps and to make sure that all aspects of each step have been examined. Checklists may represent a consensus while assuring the user that most relevant factors have been considered and that all necessary actions have been taken. Overall, checklists represent a logical-analytical framework—an attempt to ensure that everything concerning the problem will be taken into consideration (which is deemed necessary) before reaching a decision.

Specific types of checklists that have been developed to facilitate creative thinking about problems include:

- *word simulation*—uses lists of words to scan ideas and suggestions that spark creativity in the minds of those trying to solve the problem.
- *attribute listing*—identifies all the attributes or characteristics of a problem and examines each in turn.
- *area thinking*—uses three or four major areas of consideration in a problem as starting points, then works toward detail in each area. It is the oppposite of attribute listing.
- *Osborn's checklist*—lists words, such as magnify, substitute, and re-arrange, that can be used in sequence to consider alternatives to each subsection of a problem.

A summary of the problem-finding techniques for corporate planning is found in Figure 2.1. It should be noted that these techniques are equally useful in the problem-solving process.

Figure 2.1
Useful problem-finding techniques for corporate planning

Creative thinking. Centers on trying new and untired approaches, including generally nonstandard approaches and methods. Creative thinking includes the period of incubation, where decision alternatives are fermenting, that finally results in the illumination stage of creative problem finding.

Brainstorming. Attempts to "storm" a problem quickly by allowing the participants to suggest off the "top" of their heads ideas concerning the problem's solution without allowing criticism.

Synectics. Attempts to teach creativity. Its purpose is to improve the quality of creative output.

Problem definition table. Utilizes a table graph to ask questions about what is and what is not, in terms of what, when, who, where, and to what extent, for defining the problem.

Checklists. Facilitates thinking about problems by using specific types of checklists—word simulation, attribute listing, area thinking, and Osborn's checklists—to ensure that everything has been taken into account.

USEFUL BACKGROUND FOR PROBLEM FINDING: THE PROBLEM-SOLVING PROCESS

Although the basic phases of the two approaches to the problem-solving process are identical—identification, solution, and implementation—they differ in that the accent of the quantitative-centered approach is on "optimizing" versus "satisficing" for the decision-centered approach. The quantitative-centered approach concentrates on the use of standard and custom-made mathematical or statistical models that are, for the most part, computer oriented to explore the innumerable possible outcomes in a structured problem environment for an optimal answer to one "what if" question. In contrast, the decision-centered approach allows the corporate planner to be at the center of the problem-solving process by asking a number of "what if" questions (rather than concentrating on a single question as in the quantitative-centered approach) as the structure dictates to solve a semistructured problem. To explore all the possibilities within a semistructured environment and compare them on the same basis for an optimal answer would be too costly and time consuming using a quantitative-centered approach. The need for satisficing, then, is necessary in such an environment. The word *satisficing* means finding and selecting a satisfactory alternative (as opposed to the best one) that achieves a minimally acceptable solution. In a similar manner, to try and explore all the possibilities from a long string of "what if" questions in a structured problem environment would also constitute high costs and extreme time demands on the corporate planner. Again, there is need for satisficing in such situations. If the problem structures are more difficult than those posed by a structured or a semistructured environment—that is, unstructured—the decision-centered approach would be a more logical one for reaching a final solution than that of the quantitative-centered approach.

All in all, the two approaches to decision making recognize the difficulties of assessing the real world as it actually is. If a structured problem within the business environment is simple to complex and allows the corporate planner to have control over the problem-solving process, it may well be that a quantitative-centered approach is the one to be used to solve the problem at hand. On the other hand, if the problem is semistructured or unstructured, generally the best approach to use is the decision-centered approach. In any event, the attendant circumstances should be surveyed for the appropriate approach.

Quantitative-Centered Approach

The quantitative-centered approach, which is the extension of the scientific method, centers on the following steps: (1) observation, (2) definition of the problem, (3) formulation of a hypothesis, (4) experimentation, and (5) verification. These steps have been altered to accommodate the ever-changing business environment. The current steps for the quantitative-centered approach are shown in Figure 2.2. These nine steps are seldom, if ever, conducted in a particular order since there is usually a constant interplay among the steps. However, these steps provide a conceptual framework for problem solving.

To establish control over the solution, it is necessary to establish a monitoring system, preferably as a part of a computerized management information system, that will permit *feedback* to the various managers who are responsible and accountable. Continuous monitoring through feedback provides a means for modifying the solution as external-internal conditions and demands change over time. If changes are necessary, the quantitative-centered approach should be initiated, starting again with the first step.

Figure 2.2
The quantitative-centered approach within
a problem-solving environment

Steps 1–3 refer to problem *identification*.

Step 1. **Determination of objective(s) to be achieved.** Centers on the determination of the objective (or objectives) to be achieved which relates to the entire company or to one or more functional areas or to one or more activities. Overall, the objective defines what is to be accomplished in general terms. In turn, the derivative objectives focus on more detail; that is, *what* is to be accomplished, *where* action is to take place, *who* is to perform it, *how* it is to be undertaken, and *when* it is to be accomplished.

Step 2. **Observation.** Starts with the observation of the phenomena surrounding the problem—the facts, opinions, symptoms, and so on. Observation may be a casual glance or a concentrated, detailed, and lengthy study, depending on the requirements of the problem. Basically, this step is used to identify problems.

Step 3. **Definition of the real problem.** Relates to ignoring the symptoms of the problem and defining the actual problem that is impeding the accomplishment of one or more desired objectives. To define the real problem, it is necessary to deepen one's knowledge by discussing the matter with people from whom the problem solver can really learn.

Steps 4–6 refer to problem *solution*.

Step 4. **Collect and forecast information, including making assumptions.** Concerned with a forward look at the environment that is anticipated. These forecasts and assessments should be made in terms of the external and internal environmental factors. Similarly, assumptions play an important role since they provide a basis for the development of courses of action.

Step 5. **Development and evaluation of alternative solutions.** Relates not so much to developing alternative courses of action, but rather lies in reducing the alternatives so that the more promising ones can be analyzed. Even with computer-oriented quantitative models, there still can be a problem. As alternative courses of action are developed, many of the previous steps may need to be refined or reconsidered.

Step 6. **Selection of optimal solution.** Centers on the selection of the most desirable solution and development of its subparts. If the future state of the economy is uncertain, analysis and evaluation of alternatives may indicate that rather than one course several courses of action are to be followed.

Steps 7–9 refer to *implementation*.

Step 7. **Employment of sensitivity analysis.** A way of observing output changes while varying inputs to determine their relative impact on the solution. In essence, it is helpful to know how "sensitive" the solution is to changes in the values of key factors.

Step 8. **Verification of optimal solution.** Necessary because the reaction of competitors, consumer buying habits, and comparable factors observed in the limited sample during the development of the alternative courses of action and the selection of the optimal solution may not hold true for the target population.

Step 9. **Establishment of proper controls over solution.** Concerned with the solution remaining an optimal one. The solution goes out of control when one or more of the factors and/or or more of the relationships have changed significantly.

Decision-Centered Approach

In the quantitative-centered approach to the problem-solving process, the problem solver tries to choose the best or "optimal" alternative, that is, one that balances the costs, benefits, and uncertainties and is therefore most likely to achieve the most satisfactory results. Optimizing a decision means making the best one available to the company at a given time. In practice, important information may be lacking, the individual may be under pressure to act quickly and with apparent decisiveness, or the individual may have overlooked alternatives in the early stages of the problem-solving process. These limitations restrict decision making and, thereby, result in *satisficing*. However, there is a word of caution. Problem solvers should not select the first satisfactory alternative developed but should take the opportunity and time to develop other feasible alternatives.

An essential part of satisficing is the concept of *bounded rationality*. The fact that problem solvers often make decisions without knowing all the alternatives available to them and their possible consequences means that there is a limit to how logical or rational their decisions can be. In everyday organizational life, they make the most logical decisions they can, limited by their inadequate information and by their ability to utilize that information, thereby resulting in bounded rationality.[1] Within bounded rationality, rather than make the best or ideal decision, problem solvers more realistically settle for a decision that will "satisfice" rather than "optimize."

This satisficing approach does not mean that managers should give up trying to make the best possible decisions. It simply means that they recognize that at some point it is too expensive, time consuming, or difficult to acquire additional information or attempt to analyze it. For example, it is more practical for a finance manager to try to decide what must be done to earn an "acceptable" level of profits rather than try to "maximize" potential profits. Similarly, it is more practical for a marketing manager to select a product name from several good alternatives rather than examine all possible alternatives.

In light of business world realities, Herbert Simon's three steps of problem solving are intelligence, design, and choice.[2] Additionally, other steps can be appended. A revised ordering of the decision-centered approach and its essential contents are given in Figure 2.3. As with the quantitative-centered approach, there is need for feedback which may signal the need to start the process anew.

Figure 2.3
**The decision-centered approach within
a problem-solving environment**

Step 1 refers to problem *identification*.

Step 1. **Intelligence.** Concerned with searching the environment for conditions calling for decisions; that is, problem recognition. It is basically a data-gathering phase in which the problem solver seeks information to define more clearly the problem and provide some input to the solution process

Steps 2 and 3 refer to problem *solution*.

Step 2. **Design.** Centers on inventing, developing, and analyzing possible courses of action. It involves manipulation of the data obtained to develop various alternative solutions to the problem. The individual's perception of the problem is used as the data are assembled and manipulated to provide input in the development of alternatives.

Step 3. **Choice.** Centers on evaluating alternatives. This phase of the problem-solving process also requires selection of the best from among the alternatives developed in the design phase. The choice may be made under a satisficing perspective or even from an optimization perspective.

Steps 4–6 refer to *implementation*.

Step 4. **Sensitivity analysis.** Centers on the employment of sensitivity analysis; that is, observing output changes while varying inputs to determine their relative impact on the final solution. As in the seventh step of the quantitative-centered approach, typically a person engages in sensitivity analysis when asking "what if" questions.

Step 5. **Implementation.** Puts the chosen solution into effect. In effect, the best alternative selected in Step 3 and analyzed further in Step 4 is placed into operation for better or for worse. If a good alternative has been selected, the results will be favorable. If, on the other hand, a poor alternative has been implemented, the results generally will show this condition. This step parallels the eighth step of the quantitative-centered approach.

Step 6. **Control.** Involves the monitoring of the outcome and making the necessary adjustments. In essence, this step links back to the first step, namely intelligence, by recognizing a new problem that needs to be solved. This step is like the last one of the quantitative-centered approach.

PROBLEM-CENTERED APPROACH
TO PROBLEM FINDING

Because the steps for the problem-centered approach to problem finding are not currently found in the business literature, there is need to develop the appropriate steps. The approach set forth below consists of four steps plus the solution and implementation phases from the problem-solving process (the quantitative-centered approach or the decision-centered approach). These steps are related to a corporate planning example in the next section of the chapter.

Step 1. Generation

This initial step is the most important one for the basic phase of search. It focuses on the probing for potential problems that might exist in the future which would have a great impact on the company. First, the analysis is "forward looking" because this is a search for future problems. Once these problems are identified, the analysis becomes "backward looking" since there is a need to evaluate the cause-effect relationships of each problem and its possible effects on the company currently. Accent is placed on each problem as it affects the planning—from the short range to the long range. In addition, it may be necessary to look at each problem in different economic climates, in good, average, and bad conditions.

The best approach to generate important problems at the highest level, for example, is to utilize the well-known brainstorming approach for a problem-finding group. Typically, top management and its staff, along with members from the corporate planning staff, meet periodically to "brainstorm" future company problems. In such a session, all important company problems are recorded. An analysis is performed which gives the important aspects of each problem. The original question concerning the problem as *given* and the subsequent spontaneous ideas are all written down. When participants' minds have cleared, they concentrate on reformulations which are produced from the collected material and a choice of one or more is made before continuing with questions in sequence concerning the problem as *understood*. As noted above, the analysis which is initially "forward looking" becomes "backward looking." This can be repeated until all aspects have been considered. Rather complex problems may need other creativity techniques in order to approach them from an unexpected, new angle.

Step 2. Evaluation

After the problem-generation phase, there is an examination of the problems in terms of their being valid or invalid for managerial concern. Because many of these problems are found in the future—the next two to ten years—a general question can be asked of top management and corporate planners, "Which problem or problems should be undertaken for solution?" To answer this question, there is need to evaluate what impact the solution of a problem has on the company, such as in terms of net profit before federal income taxes and return on investment. In other cases, consideration might be given to other important areas of a company, such as impact on the company's sales and customer service.

In most situations, there is need to utilize a *cost-benefit analysis* to determine what impact solving the problem has on the financial aspects of the company today and tomorrow. This task, for example, can be relegated to the corporate planning staff to determine those problems that are of valid concern for managerial action. The problems generated in Step 1, then, are evaluated in terms of benefits versus costs, thereby becoming the basis for validation in the next step.

These first two steps of the problem-centered approach are related to the search for problems. The remaining steps are associated with identification, solution, and implementation.

Step 3. Validation

Building upon the prior step of problem evaluation, actual problems are selected as being worthy of managerial concern for today and tomorrow. The validation for solving these problems is generally backed up by a cost-benefit analysis. If such an analysis is not available or too difficult or costly to develop, it may be necessary to use alternative means, such as the consensus of the majority of the problem-finding group, to substantiate this selection as an important problem to be solved. As in Step 1, a brainstorming approach may be necessary "to get a handle" on problems that cannot be quantified.

For example, to determine what problems should be validated and solved, the problem-finding group meets again and reviews the recommendations of the corporate planning staff. For the most part, the staff has prioritized the important problems to be solved. It is up to the problem-finding group to pass judgment on them. As noted above, some of the problems cannot be resolved in terms of a cost-benefit analysis. Input from corporate planners is generally necessary to finalize the prioritized list for implementation.

Step 4. Establish Boundaries

Once the problems have been validated, it is necessary to describe or define each problem within its boundaries. This ensures that areas that the problem might touch upon or come into contact with will be included in the problem-finding process. The net result is that there is need for some fine-tuning such that the appropriate boundaries which the problem encompasses will be considered in its solution. Typically, to establish realistic boundaries, the problem-finding group must have a good knowledge of the future (good, average, or poor economic conditions), a clear description of performance that a solution must fulfill, and a clear idea of what to expect from solving the problem. These areas must be as clear and accurate as possible, because when the problem is badly defined, the solution is generally of no value to management. The GIGO (Garbage-In, Garbage-Out) principle is found in such cases.

Steps 3 and 4 of the problem-centered approach center on problem identification. These steps are to be followed by those relating to solution and implementation.

Steps 5 and 6. Solution

The solution to the problem-centered approach can take one of two directions. One is the use of Step 5 (Development and Evaluation of Alternative Solutions) and Step 6 (Selection of Optimal

Solution), as found in the quantitative-centered approach (Figure 2.2). The other is the use of Step 2 (Design) and Step 3 (Choice) as found in the decision-centered approach (Figure 2.3). The proper approach is dictated by the type of future problems being solved. In either case, the solution centers on solving future problems before they actually occur. The accent is on practicing management by perception versus the traditional management by exception found in problem solving.

Steps 7, 8, and 9. Implementation

In these final steps for the problem-centered approach, the implementation steps for the problem-solving process are usable (as noted in Figures 2.2 and 2.3). Fundamentally, these steps for the quantitative-centered approach and the decision-centered approach are the same. An integral part of implementation is establishing control over the solution in order to detect how changing times are affecting the solution.

The preceding nine steps, as set forth in Figure 2.4, are generally conducted in the order as presented. However, there may be circumstances that warrant changing the above sequence. As in the problem-solving process, there is need of feedback in the problem-centered approach.

Figure 2.4
The problem-centered approach within a
problem-finding environment

Steps 1 and 2 refer to problem *search.*

Step 1. **Generation.** Probe for potential problems that might exist in the future which have a great impact on the company. A popular approach is to utilize the brainstorming approach. The analysis which is initially "forward looking" becomes a "backward-looking" approach.

Step 2. **Evaluation.** Review problems uncovered in terms of validity for managerial concern. In most situations, there is need to utilize a cost-benefit analysis to determine what impact the problem has on the company.

Steps 3 and 4 refer to problem *identification.*

Step 3. **Validation.** An extension of problem evaluation in that one or more actual problems are validated for managerial concern. The validation is generally backed up by a cost-benefit analysis. If such an analysis is not available, alternative means are needed to substantiate this selection of problem(s).

Step 4. **Establish boundaries.** Define each potential problem within its boundaries so as to cover the whole area that the problem encompasses. There may be need for fine-tuning so that the appropriate boundaries are established.

Steps 5 and 6. **Solution.** Use Steps 5 and 6 of the quantitative-centered approach or Steps 2 and 3 of the decision-centered approach to the problem-solving process (refer to Figures 2.2 and 2.3).

Steps 7, 8, and 9. **Implementation.** Use Steps 7, 8, and 9 of the quantitative-centered approach or Steps 4, 5, and 6 of the decision-centered approach to the problem-solving process (refer to Figures 2.2 or 2.3).

CORPORATE PLANNING EXAMPLE OF PROBLEM-CENTERED APPROACH TO PROBLEM FINDING

To illustrate the problem-centered approach, the president of the XYZ Corporation wants the corporate planning staff to examine its operations from an overview standpoint—from five to six years hence. In view of this mandate, the first step (generation) centers on a probe for potential problems which possibly could exist in later years. Of great importance to the corporate planners is the evaluation of the corporation's forthcoming products over the next five to six years. A brainstorming approach regarding future sales potential pinpoints that the corporation is depending too much on variations of present products rather than on new products. In essence, the XYZ Corporation will be losing its market share, especially in the fifth and sixth years. As a result of lost market share, administrative overhead, as well as many manufacturing and marketing expenses, will be higher than normal due to the reduced volume. Other problems center on the current expansion of capacity at its manufacturing plants, not to mention the current emphasis on expanding the current sales force. Additionally, the problem of improving service to meet competition can be identified over the next several years.

In the second step (evaluation), the above problems are evaluated thoroughly by the corporate planning staff from the standpoint of being valid or invalid for management's concern. In addition, each problem needs to be viewed form the standpoint of benefits to be derived from its solution versus costs incurred to solve it. These first two steps are directed toward problem search.

In the third step (validation) of the problem-centered approach, the important problems encountered by the corporate planning staff are validated for managerial concern. The benefits to be derived and the costs to be incurred are examined in more detail for accuracy and completeness. A cost-benefit analysis for solving each problem, then, quantifies the magnitude of each problem confronting the corporate planners. For example, the benefits of relying too heavily on variations of the present product line over the next five to six years in terms of sales are related to costs incurred for these sales. In addition, other factors that cannot be quantified should be included with the cost-benefit analysis. As an example, consider the level of customer service, which is very difficult to quantify. Typically, several major problems will be validated by the corporate planning staff. The major ones that center on marketing, manufacturing, and overhead have been identified above.

Moving on to the fourth step (establish boundaries), each of the problems is described within its normal limits as determined by the corporate planning staff. For the manufacturing problem, its boundaries might be restricted in terms of manufacturing locations to the United States only versus several or all countries of the world. These second two steps focus on problem identification.

Now that the problems have been adequately explored and defined, the solution to each of these problems reverts back to either the quantitative-centered approach or the decision-centered approach. Due to the semistructured nature of the problems—caused by the long time frame over five to six years—the decision-centered approach is used to solve them.

However, the attendant circumstances must be examined for each problem to determine the appropriate solution method. Overall, the solution to the problems and their implementation conclude the steps in this problem-centered illustration.

OPPORTUNITY-CENTERED APPROACH TO PROBLEM FINDING

As with the preceding approach, the opportunity-centered approach to the problem-finding process has not been identified in definitive terms in the business literature. Although no formal steps have been developed to date, recommended steps for the opportunity-centered approach are given below. They entail three steps plus the addition of the solution and implementation phases from the problem-solving process. (See Figure 2.5.)

Step 1. Exploration

This initial step examines the external and internal environmental factors for opportunities that arise when problems are uncovered. The focus is directed away from the short range to the medium range and long range. Fundamentally, there is a corporate planning effort to determine what opportunities are presented by the problems uncovered in the future. The analysis is initially forward looking in that there is a search for future problems. Once the problems have been identified, they are examined from the standpoint of identifying opportunities for improving the company's operations (whether it be from the standpoint of sales, profits, or otherwise). From this perspective, the concept of opportunities has a "positive" connotation, while the concept of problems has a "negative" one. As in the problem-centered approach, brainstorming is generally used by top management and the corporate planning staff. This first step can also be referred to as the search for possible opportunities.

Step 2. Selection

Once opportunities have been identified, the next step is to determine what opportunities (one or more) should be explored

Figure 2.5
The opportunity-centered approach within a
problem-finding environment

Step 1 refers to a *search* for possible opportunities.

Step 1. **Exploration.** Examine the environment for opportunities that
come from problems uncovered. Generally, a brainstorming
approach is used by top management and the corporate planning staff.

Steps 2 and 3 refer to opportunity *identification*.

Step 2. **Selection.** Determine that one or more opportunities should be
explored by top management and corporate planners. The selection process should focus on those opportunities that relate
to a company's *critical success factors* (factors that are critical
to its success).

Step 3. **Examine boundaries.** Survey the environment for each opportunity and determine the proper boundaries. Due to the nature
of some opportunities, the boundaries may be quite wide.

Steps 4 and 5. **Solution.** Use Steps 5 and 6 of the quantitative-centered
approach or Steps 2 and 3 of the decision-centered approach to
the problem-solving process (refer to Figures 2.2 and 2.3).

Steps 6, 7, and 8. **Implementation.** Use Steps 7, 8, and 9 of the quantitative-centered approach of Steps 4, 5, and 6 of the decision-
centered approach to the problem-solving process (refer to
Figures 2.2 and 2.3).

---

by top management and corporate planners. The selection process should focus on those opportunities that relate to a company's *critical success factors*—that is, those factors that are
critical to its success (to be explored in more depth in Chapter 6).
Typically, these factors include price, sales promotion, customer
service, product mix, inventory turnover, cost control, and
quality dealers. In turn, the interrelationships of the critical
success factors and the company's goals and objectives are discussed for further clarification. But more important, this discussion determines what opportunities should be pursued by the
company, thereby identifying them in a clear and meaningful
way. Moreover, it takes into consideration all the important
facts that bear on important company opportunities. Where

deemed necessary, a cost-benefit analysis can be used to determine what opportunities are more important than others in terms of how they affect the company's future profits and return on investment.

Step 3. Examine Boundaries

In this step, there is need to survey the environment for the opportunities identified before pursuing an opportunity solution. Due to the nature of some opportunities, the boundaries may be quite wide; that is, they extend beyond the company and are related to emerging and established organizations and industries. Typically, greater opportunities exist when boundaries are extended than when boundaries are very narrow. Thus, it behooves top management and its corporate planning staff to examine the boundaries surrounding the opportunities from a narrow to a very large perspective. The net result is that the proper boundaries are used in the solution and implementation of the opportunity. Steps 2 and 3 are referred to as opportunity identification.

Steps 4 and 5. Solution

As in the problem-centered approach, the solution in the opportunity-centered approach can take one of two directions—the quantitative-centered approach (Figure 2.2) or the decision-centered approach (Figure 2.3). Fundamentally, current problem-solving approaches require that the problem solver pick the best solution from the set of feasible ones. The main thrust is on practicing management by perception.

Steps 6, 7, and 8. Implementation

For these last steps of the opportunity-centered approach, the implementation steps for the problem-solving process are used (refer to Figures 2.2 and 2.3). More specifically, there is need for implementing the opportunity as well as monitoring the opportunity, thereby making the necessary adjustments to changing times.

As with the problem-centered approach, the steps in the

opportunity-centered approach are linked to certain basic phases of the problem-solving process. As before, feedback is necessary, providing a means for recognizing new opportunities.

CORPORATE PLANNING EXAMPLE OF OPPORTUNITY-CENTERED APPROACH TO PROBLEM FINDING

To demonstrate this approach for the XYZ Corporation, an aggressive long-term strategy of adding new sales offices (approximately two per year) has been undertaken around the country where population growth warrants them. Based upon this strategy, projections were made by the corporate planning staff to determine if this was a viable approach over the next five to six years. Due to shifting population trends, some northern and midwestern cities would no longer be able to support sales offices. Thus, a major problem that needs to be addressed today was identified in specific areas of the country.

Although the foregoing analysis did not provide solutions, it did identify the need for corporate management to get involved with the corporate planning staff in an extensive planning effort in order to determine what opportunities exist for the sales office problem. Opportunities were explored by using a brainstorming approach and important opportunities were identified, such as expanding the company's product line so that these marginal sales offices could remain open. Other opportunities took the form of working with another company having a similar problem or merging with another company. Overall, the first step (exploration)—examining the environment for opportunities that come from problems uncovered—was undertaken. This first step is directed toward opportunity search.

For the second step (selection), top managers and their corporate planning staff directed their efforts initially at identifying those factors critical to the company's success. They were identified to be (1) good product mix, (2) fast inventory turnover, (3) effective cost control over manufacturing and service operations, and (4) competitive price. The sales office situation is linked directly or indirectly to these factors. To select the opportunity to follow, it was decided to use a cost-benefit analysis approach that included giving consideration to the intangible factors related to the sales offices. The outcome was that the company would explore the feasibility of working with or merging with another company experiencing a similar sales office problem in the future.

In the third step (examining boundaries), the working with or merging with another company could relate to those firms in the same industry or dissimilar industries. Also, consideration should be given to those companies that operate throughout the United States only.

Steps 2 and 3 have focused on opportunity identification. Now that the opportunity has been adequately identified, a good answer to the various ways of resolving this opportunity reverts back to either the quantitative-centered approach or a decison-centered approach. Due to the structure and long-term nature of the opportunity, the decision-centered approach is generally a logical choice. If other opportunities were identified to be solved, the quantitative-centered approach might be more appropriate. The solution to the opportunity and its implementation represent the final steps in the opportunity-centered approach.

OVERVIEW OF PROBLEM-CENTERED AND OPPORTUNITY-CENTERED APPROACHES TO PROBLEM FINDING

Even though the basic phases of the two approaches (refer to Figures 2.4 and 2.5) are the same—that is, search, identification, solution, and implementation—they differ in that the main thrust of the problem-centered approach is on identifying future problems and determining appropriate solutions today to minimize their impact on the company. In contrast, the opportunity-centered approach goes a step further by not only identifying future problems but also determining what opportunities exist to overcome these problems. This orientation is a very positive one. The major accent is on improving operations as opposed to focusing exclusively on finding where operations can go wrong in the future.

For both approaches, mathematical and statistical models are employed to support the problem-finding process. Typically, there is a great reliance on heuristic methods due to the fact that not all variables can be identified and defined, and those that can cannot always be quantified. As they arise in the normal course of using either approach, numerous questions can be answered in a computerized mode using quantitative models. Irregardless of the problem structure, answers can be given today not only to pinpoint future problems and opportunities but also to determine their impact on the functional areas to which they are related. In summary, the problem- and opportunity-centered approaches are of great assistance to top management and corporate planners for obtaining an overview of where the company stands today and tomorrow as well as showing specific interrelationships of functional areas. Failure to deploy problem finding may result in the implementation of a corporate strategy that will produce less than desired results.

SUMMARY

The main focus of this chapter was on the problem-finding process which can be categorized into the problem-centered approach and the opportunity-centered approach. The basic phases of the problem-finding process include search, identification, solution, and implementation. Generally, this process is used to solve semistructured and unstructured problems with a time frame beyond one year. Typically, the time frame is several years, particularly five years, which ties in with strategic planning. Additionally, this chapter demonstrated the use of both approaches to problem finding for the XYZ Corporation—a typical business organization. In future chapters, real-world examples will be given for applying the problem-finding process.

NOTES

1. Herbert A. Simon, *Models of Man: Social and Rational* (New York: John Wiley & Sons, 1957).

2. Herbert A. Simon, *The New Science of Management Decisions* (New York: Harper & Row, 1960), pp. 2-3.

3

Decision Support Systems and Problem Finding

Utilizes Management by Perception

Human-Machine Interface

Facilitates the Decision Maker's Reasoning Process

Easy-to-Use Approach

Supports Decision Making for Solving All Types of Problem Structures

Use of Mathematical/Statistical Models and Modeling Languages

Adaptive System over Time

Overview of Decision Support Systems

Decision Support System for a Typical Organization

Corporate Planning Example of Using a Decision Support System to Assist in Problem Finding: Savin Corporation

Summary

To facilitate the implementation of the problem-finding process (and the problem-solving process), this chapter looks at the use of an important direction in management information systems, namely, decision support systems (DSS). This computerized approach is a way of formalizing decision making at the higher levels in a business organization. More specifically, decision support systems are an effective means to assist corporate planners in everyday decision making. Not only are they "user friendly," but they are readily adaptable to changing environmental (external and internal) factors. From this perspective, the essentials of decision support systems are discussed along with a typical application. In addition, a corporate planning example—the Savin Corporation—demonstrates the use of a DSS operating mode to assist in problem finding. Before exploring the essentials of decision support systems, the relationship of problem finding to effective corporate planning within a DSS environment along with the information needs of top, middle, and lower management are examined.

THE RELATIONSHIP OF PROBLEM FINDING TO EFFECTIVE CORPORATE PLANNING WITHIN A DECISION SUPPORT SYSTEM ENVIRONMENT

To undertake a more effective job of corporate planning, it is helpful to make problem finding an integral part of a decision support system. This can be accomplished in several ways. A straightforward way is to utilize a personal computer along with appropriate DSS software packages. Another typical way is to employ a computer mainframe with appropriate software capable of providing answers to a wide range of problems. However, a newer way for top management and corporate planners is to utilize large display devices that are capable of showing operating and financial information for today and tomorrow. Such a decision-making environment can be called either a "management control center" or a "decision room."

The importance of this last way lies in its ability to call up a wide variety of management information for problem finding. Instead of searching files and cluttering up the office with paperwork, executives and corporate planners can view the required information together in one room. They can, for example, obtain sales figures for any time period, together with comparable figures for previous periods. Current production schedules, the number of pending orders, status of back orders, amounts of accounts receivable, profit analysis by periods and products, equipment utilization, and divisional performance factors are additional examples of available information that may be helpful in problem finding.

These uses by no means exhaust the information from a management control center. Problem finding information will always be current, accurate, and in a form well suited for fast evaluation. Graphs, charts, and indexes on the large display screen will keep information to a minimum, thereby increasing management's and corporate planners' understanding. Pages and pages of tabular information can be condensed into one projected display picture. Exception reporting will also reduce the amount of data for possible viewing, and the use of computer-generated displays will further reduce the need for paper reporting. Thus, the speed and simplification of reporting will allow top management and corporate planners time to interact with computer output to determine future problems and related opportunities confronting the company in terms of problem finding.

INFORMATION NEEDS FOR DECISION MAKING WITHIN A DSS ENVIRONMENT

Within the framework of decision support systems, it is helpful to examine the information needs of top, middle, and lower management. Generally, top management and corporate planners are concerned with *strategic information* while *tactical information* and *operational information* are useful to middle and lower management, respectively. The type of information supplied also has to do with the activities with which the information is concerned—the internal environment of the company and the external environment in which the company operates.

It is generally recognized that internal information should be more and more summarized as the level of management for which it is prepared rises in the hierarchical structure, with top management receiving overall reports of operations for future planning. On the other hand, lower echelons of management, being control oriented, receive the most detailed reports. Between top and lower management is middle management, which is planning-control oriented. All three levels of informational needs are illustrated in Figure 3.1.

Information concerning the external environment of the company should be summarized in exactly the opposite manner from that of the internal environment. Because the upper levels are more planning oriented and because planning necessitates more information about the company's external environment, this type of information should be most fully supplied to top management. It should be increasingly summarized and selec-

Figure 3.1
Types of information reports found at the various management levels, including corporate planners, for planning and control over company activities

Management Levels	Types of Information Reports	Related To
Top management and corporate planners	Overall reports fundamentally planning oriented	Strategic information
Middle management	Comprehensive reports basically planning/ control oriented	Tactical information
Lower management	Detailed reports generally control oriented	Operational information

tive as the position of the receiver decreases in the managerial hierarchy. Time spent in planning and control for top, middle, and lower management complement one another in a computerized DSS environment, as shown in Figure 3.2.

Figure 3.2
The relationship of the management levels, including corporate planners, to time spent on planning and control

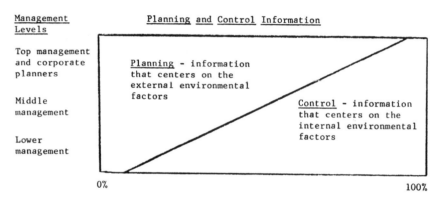

Management Levels — Planning and Control Information

Top management and corporate planners

Middle management

Lower management

Planning - information that centers on the external environmental factors

Control - information that centers on the internal environmental factors

0%   100%

Strategic Information for Top Management

Strategic information is used primarily by top management and corporate planners to cover a long time span—generally beyond one year on up to five years and beyond (if deemed necessary). This type of information is employed for planning purposes and for the analysis of problem areas to discover the underlying reasons for specific problems or conditions. In many cases, the objective of strategic information is to find answers to the question *why* rather than what or where. Examples include the design of new products, the optimal allocation of present manufacturing facilities as well as projected financial statements for five years, and a determination of future long-term capital needs from outside services.

Planning must occur before strategic information can be gathered. Strategic planning concerns itself with establishing goals and objectives as well as policies that will govern the acquisition, use, and distribution of the resources needed to achieve these goals and objectives. It is normally conducted at the highest level of management and will consist of a very broad level of detail. Primarily, it requires large amounts of information derived from or relating to areas of knowledge outside of the company. Finally, strategic planning is original and covers the entire spectrum of the company's activities. This area of strategic planning as well as tactical and operational information is summarized in Figure 3.3.

Figure 3.3
A summary of information needs for decision making
within a DSS environment

Strategic information. Covers one to five years and beyond (if deemed necessary) and is used by top management and corporate planners for *planning* purposes. Its primary sources lie outside the company.

Tactical information. Covers longer time periods (up to one year) than operational information and is *planning-control* oriented. It is used by middle management to implement strategic plans at the functional levels.

Operational information. Concerned with structured and repetitive activities of today, next week, and next month that are measurable in terms of specific results. This type of information is *control* oriented and is needed by lower-level managers, such as plant foremen and department heads.

Tactical Information for Middle Management

Tactical information that covers relatively short time periods (not greater than twelve months) is used by middle management to implement the highest-level strategic plans at the functional levels. Typically, tactical information is used by a large number of people. Examples are a functional budget report that compares actual to estimated amounts, a production report that evaluates assembly operations, alternative investment opportunities for return on short-term assets, and a vendor performance report that evaluates overall vendor performance.

Operational Information for Lower Management

Operational information, being at the lowest level, is concerned with structured and repetitive activities today, next week, and next month that are measurable in terms of specific results. It allows the company's line managers, such as plant foremen and department heads, to measure performance against predetermined goals, including standards and budgeted figures. Similarly, operational information allows lower management to comment on how operating standards and policies can be improved to assist day-to-day operations. Feedback of essential information from this low level keeps higher management levels aware of unfavorable as well as favorable results. Typical examples of operational information include open sales orders, engineering specifications, uncompleted manufacturing orders, and inventory on hand.

THE ESSENTIALS OF DECISION SUPPORT SYSTEMS

To satisfy the information needs of management and corporate planners in a "future" environment, the need arose for a new direction in management information systems or decision support systems. Fundamentally, decision support systems are systems designed to support the decision-making process of managers and support personnel. They incorporate features found in prior management information systems and employ mathematical and statistical models found in the discipline of management science (that is, operations research). They emphasize direct support to enhance the professional judgment required in making decisions, especially when the problem structures tend to be semistructured and unstructured. Emphasis is placed on helping the individual make decisions rather than on actually making decisions as found in prior management information systems. This interplay results in a total effort that is greater than the individual or the computer operating independently, thereby providing *synergistic* decision making. Only selected information is presented, as opposed to presenting all information that might be useful. From this perspective, decision support systems build upon as well as complement present management information systems. This relationship is illustrated in Figure 3.4.

Figure 3.4
Comparison of problem structure and decision-making capability for prior management information systems and decision support systems

Type of System	Problem Structure	Decision-Making Capability
Prior Management Information Systems	Well structured	New information produced using analytical techniques for specific decision-making situations Summarization of information in the form of control reports
Decision Support Systems	Semistructured and unstructured along with well structured	Manager-machine interface where the manager retains control over the decision-making process Synergistic decision making

Utilizes Management by Perception

Within a DSS environment, the management-by-perception principle is used. As already noted, this principle refers to the ability of management to perceive the future before it occurs and to determine its impact on the organization now. It represents a forward-looking approach as opposed to the backward-looking approach of management by exception which focuses on comparison after the fact. However, it should be pointed out that both have their place in a DSS operating mode.

Human-Machine Interface

A fundamental characteristic of decision support systems is the human-machine interface, whereby the decision maker (corporate planner) retains control throughout the problem-finding and problem-solving processes. This approach not only results in bringing decision-making information directly to the decision maker but also goes a step further than typical management information systems by allowing the individual to react to the output. Hence, the decision maker can react with the computer by getting many answers, rather than just one answer, to a series of "what if" questions. In this manner, the computer does not have the final say in the problem-finding or problem-solving process but is simply a tool of the decision maker for evaluating alternatives so that an effective decision can be made.

The focus of the human-machine interface is on learning, creativity, and evaluation rather than on replacement, automation, and routine procedures. A DSS approach allows the decision maker to look inside a problem to see what makes it "tick." When doing so, the decision maker will discover new aspects of the problem that were not obvious before. The individual will want to isolate certain parameters and ask a series of "what if" questions about these selected parameters—that is, "*What* happens to the final results *if* we change this aspect of the problem?" This interplay between the decision maker and the computer gives the individual a new way of arriving at answers to problems.

Facilitates the Decision Maker's Reasoning Process

To utilize the capabilities of DSS to their fullest, query capabilities exist that assist the decision maker (corporate planner), making the system an extension of his or her reasoning process. Models of the business environment allow one to envision possibilities for the future, foresee consequences, and evaluate alternative solutions. Based on this view, DSS provides the ability to retrieve information in such a way that meaningful patterns and correlations can be discerned. Hence, the user's reasoning process is augmented. With the use of modeling languages (to be explored below), the user can become competent in constructing and solving models in an interactive, exploratory manner that corresponds loosely to the facilities of memory and reasoning.

Going one step further, query capabilities of decision support systems should be able to support various approaches to decision making. A model of the decision-making process has been developed by Herbert Simon. He characterized three main steps in the process: (1) intelligence (searching the environment for conditions calling for decision), (2) design (inventing, developing, and analyzing possible courses of action), and (3) choice (selecting a course of action from those available). Overall, an interactive processing mode should provide the user with the capability of facilitating his or her own decision-making process.

Easy-to-Use Approach

The hallmark of an effective decision support system is its ease of use. A DSS not only should support the user in decision making via a human-machine interface but should be a natural extension of the user in problem finding or problem solving. The importance of this characteristic is underscored by the discretionary latitude the user has to develop newer approaches to finding problems and solving problems that is not normally allowed within an MIS framework. It may be that the user decides to try new ways of combining external information with internal information for finding new problems and their related opportunities as well as for solving problems that are critical to the company's operations.

By not being constrained by rigid requirements, such as those found in traditional MIS, the DSS user finds the system valuable and convenient to use for problem finding or problem solving. Successful DSS should be compatible with the user's modus operandi. The individual should feel that the system really assists rather than threatens or intimidates. The system should allow the user to pursue his or her own natural tendencies toward problem finding or problem solving. Thus, a decision support system should earn an individual's allegiance by being not only valuable and supportive but convenient and easy to use as well.

Supports Decision Making for Solving
All Types of Problem Structures

Typically, a decision support system provides assistance in decision making regardless of the type of problem encountered. Because past MIS provides decisions for many of the well-structured problems, there is a tendency for DSS to place emphasis on semistructured and unstructured decisions. However, it should be emphasized that structured decisions are provided for managers and their supporting staff in a DSS environment.

Within a DSS environment where a decision process is fully structured, computer automation is generally desirable since an appropriate mathematical or statistical model can be employed to reach a good decision. Where it is unstructured from the perspective of the decision maker, computerized mathematical/statistical models are generally inappropriate. For the most part, to reach a decision, there is need for managerial experience, know-how, intuition, and judgment. In the middle, the semistructured decision makes use of both computerized decision making and human judgment such that there is a balance between the two. For example, the investment decision process is considered to be semistructured. From one viewpoint, a systematic search through data on portfolios and securities is required which can be effected through retrieval, reports, and display via a CRT terminal using mathematical and statistical models. At the same time, the criteria for making investments for a specific portfolio need to be left to the manager's judgment. Thus, output from the computer is combined with the portfolio manager's judgment to select appropriate securities.

Use of Mathematical/Statistical Models
and Modeling Languages

An effective decision support system should utilize the appropriate mathematical or statistical model whether it is standard or custom-made, whether it is simple or complex. Using the on-line, interactive capabilities of computer terminals, managers and their support staff are able to participate in structuring some of the characteristics of the very models they will use. As part of this flexible modeling structure, managers are able to insert their own assumptions about key problem characteristics. Multiple runs are made to determine results under a variety of conditions. Thus, instead of a single optimal result from the model, several outputs are obtained to answer "what if" questions. This enables solutions to be judged by managers on a variety of criteria, including risk, robustness, and performance.

Typically, for many problems confronting managers, including corporate planners, in a DSS environment, the real world is far too complex to be completely described by a series of equations; objectives are too poorly defined and diffused to be captured precisely; and many similar complicating factors exist. It is therefore necessary either to use standard or to develop appropriate custom-made mathematical/statistical models that approximate the real world in order to make problems computationally feasible. Linear relationships, for example, may have to be employed in place of more complex nonlinear relationships, which, in fact, more closely reflect reality. Or a single fixed value may be used in place of several estimated values. In reality, some accuracy may have to be sacrificed to gain computational efficiency.

In addition to the foregoing mathematical/statistical models, DSS makes great use of modeling languages or fourth-generation programming languages. More recently, modeling languages have been developed that provide a way of answering a number of "what if" questions. For example, the Interactive Financial Planning System (IFPS) of EXECUCOM is a computerized simulation system designed for use by corporate planners in the planning process. It is CRT terminal oriented, employing an English-like modeling language for the process of problem finding and problem solving by means of "building a model." The model is developed in the form of a matrix, consisting of rows and columns. The rows (lines) represent variables and the columns represent the time periods. The IFPS model allows the user to describe how each of the variables is expected to change over time.

Adaptive System over Time

Throughout the design phase of DSS, there is a substantial amount of interaction between the user and the systems analyst.

However, the final design should allow for changing the system over time. In effect, the changeability factor is an integral part of the DSS design. This is in contrast with the traditional MIS approach where the final design is set in place for a period of time and reviewed periodically, say every three to five years, for necessary changes. Hence, a DSS design approach can be thought of as an adaptive system in which the corporate planner confronts new problems (caused by changes from a variety of sources) and, at the same time, solves these problems by adapting the system to changing conditions. This capability to effect system changes relatively quickly is an important advantage of decision support systems.

OVERVIEW OF DECISION SUPPORT SYSTEMS

The most important characteristic of decision support systems is the human-machine interface, with the user retaining control over the decision-making process. This approach not only results in bringing decision-making information directly to the user but also goes a step further than typical management information systems by allowing the individual to react to the output. Hence, the decision maker can interact with the computer by getting a number of answers, rather than just one answer, to a series of "what if" questions. In this manner, the computer does not have the final say in the decision-making process; it is simply a tool of the user for evaluating alternatives so that an effective decision can be made. The capability of the individual to retain control over the decision-making process is useful not only for solving well-structured problems but for solving semistructured and unstructured problems. Thus, decision support systems give the decision maker the ability to engage in problem finding and to solve a wide range of problems that must be confronted and resolved in an effective, economical manner.[1]

DECISION SUPPORT SYSTEM FOR A
TYPICAL ORGANIZATION

To highlight the differences between the MIS approach and a DSS approach, consider a production planning manager who relies on a mathematical scheduling model to plan manufacturing operations. In turn, the output from this model is also used to control day-to-day operations. Although this approach has worked well for planning/controlling purposes, there is always the problem of frequently received marginal orders. Marginal orders are defined as those received at less than full sales price from customers. In the past, they have been refused for the most part, especially if the factory is busy. However, in a DSS operating mode, the production planning manager can use a mathematical scheduling model via a CRT terminal to determine the effect of making changes to the present schedule in terms of end completion dates. Using a human machine interface, if changes can be made to the production schedule such that present shipping dates can be met and there is a contribution toward fixed costs from the marginal order(s), the acceptability or nonacceptability of such an order(s) can be established. Likewise, counterproposals can be made to customers if the sales price is too low or there is need to accept a later shipping date. In this example, the decision maker—that is, the production planning manager—has complete control over marginal orders. (See Figure 3.5 which illustrates this DSS approach.)

CORPORATE PLANNING EXAMPLE OF USING A DECISION SUPPORT SYSTEM TO ASSIST IN PROBLEM FINDING: SAVIN CORPORATION

At the Savin Corporation, DSS efforts started with System W (a fourth-generation programming language available from Comshare, Inc.), first on a time-sharing basis and then on-line.[2] System W has proved to be an effective tool since it enables users to present information clearly, by using a flexible "record writer" that has the power to generate graphics along with text and data. It has allowed the corporation to optimize decisions by using "what if" analysis and "goal seeking" (reverse of "what if" analysis) along with iterations and variations on the data.

Essentially, what the System W DSS has done for Savin is to help the corporation move away from the traditional organization approach where people sit around a table, discuss forecasts, review sales data, and evaluate the business climate. Under that

Figure 3.5
A decision support system utilizing interactive decision making to answer "what if" questions for a production planning manager

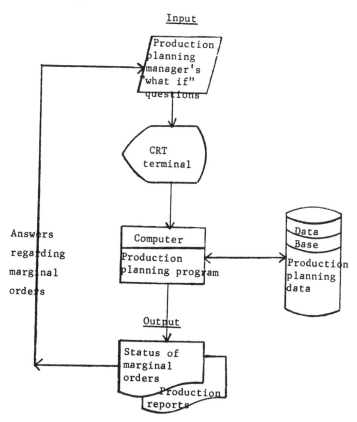

kind of operation, a lot depends on the notes and interpretation of the minutes-taker, as well as the memories of the other participants. In going the DSS route, the corporation wanted to get away from such a subjective and often inaccurate process and rely instead on a more statistically oriented approach.

To illustrate Savin's approach to DSS, it recently developed a Sales Tracking and Review Systems (STARS) approach to monitoring sales productivity. STARS is a specific example of what kind of sales data gets into the decision support system and how the DSS is used to support field representatives. Sales representatives now report their daily activities for input into the DSS. The numbers include new calls, "good" situations identified, appointments set, machine demonstrations given, orders signed, total net revenue, trials with conditional orders, and trials cancelled without an order. Each week, the sales managers receive printouts of their sales teams' activities and results for the period. Almost instantly, each manager can identify trouble spots. A low score on "new calls" might lead to a mediocre showing next month, and a poor ratio of demonstrations to sales closings might mean that a retraining program for sales representatives is in order. In effect, with numbers updated daily, the effect of such close monitoring is to take much of the guesswork out of managing.

Problem Solving in the Short Run. Going beyond solving this type of problem, Savin has a difficult planning problem in the area of inventory. Because Savin does not manufacture its copiers, it has to live within its manufacturer's time frame. Thus, it must determine how many machines it can sell, order them, and then wait eight to nine months for delivery. To place this planning problem in perspective, it can be compared to the planning process at a typical manufacturing company. Such a firm does not have any inventory in the "classic sense," that is, when the company orders something, it has a lead time of a number of months, and that is their "build cycle." Savin, by contrast, sometimes has to maintain inventories—even if it cannot move the machines—for long periods. When Savin buys for inventories, it distributes from them, and hopes that the right buying decisions have been made.

As can be seen, there is need to look at the important factors, namely, the production of suppliers, availability of machine inventories, sales forecasts, and seasonal factors. Savin marketing managers say it is basically a supply-and-demand relation: "How much will the corporation sell, how much is the corporation to forecast, and how much machine inventories are needed to make these forecasts work?" The answer was found in a decision support system by getting data faster and developing relevant information more rapidly for managers and their staff.

Problem Finding in the Long Run. Although the Savin Corporation has been successful within a DSS environment for the short run, it needs to go further and engage in problem finding for the long run. More to the point, the corporation can use the decision support system to evaluate supply and demand over the next five years. Many factors in the environment are changing independently of each other. The corporation needs a way of finding those factors and evaluating their impact and how that translates into either an increase or a decrease in machine demand. From this broad perspective, an important advantage of a problem-finding DSS is that it enables top management and corporate planners to identify the critical issues and problems involved in major decisions.

SUMMARY

Within the chapter, the accent was on decision support systems as a means to assist top management and corporate planners in fulfilling their tasks. Because these systems allow for retrieving up-to-date data from computerized files, these data can be used as input for the problem-finding process (and the problem-solving process). The end result of these systems is that important output is displayed on terminal devices (hard copy and visual) for assisting in the determination of future problems and their related opportunities. From this viewpoint, the computer's potential is more fully realized for effective corporate planning.

NOTES

1. For further information on decision support systems, see Robert J. Thierauf, *Decision Support Systems for Effective Planning and Control: A Case Study Approach* (Englewood Cliffs, N.J.: Prentice-Hall, 1982).

2. John Herman, "Savin Takes the Guesswork out of Decision Making," *Management Technology*, January 1984, p. 61.

PART II

RELATIONSHIP OF A CORPORATE PLANNER TO EFFECTIVE CORPORATE PLANNING

4

Attributes of a Corporate Planner Engaged in Problem Finding

ISSUES RAISED AND EXPLORED

- What is the relationship of an effective corporate planner to problem finding?
- What are the desired attributes of an effective corporate planner when utilizing a problem-finding approach?
- What questions can be asked to assess a corproate planner's qualifications when engaged in problem finding?
- How has a positive approach to problem finding aided management and the corporate planning staff of General Electric?

OUTLINE

An Overview: Relationship of an Effective Corporate Planner to Problem Finding

Desired Attributes of an Effective Corporate Planner Engaged in Problem Finding

    Take a Broad-Based View

    Think Strategically and Analytically

    Employ Feelings When Deemed Appropriate

    Have the Courage to Be Oneself

Be Open to Growth

Be Imaginative

Have the Capability to Fail

Recognize the Importance of Hard Work

Take a Flexible Approach

Undertake Full Responsibility

Overview of Desired Attributes for an Effective Corporate Planner

Assessing a Corporate Planner's Qualifications When Engaged in Problem Finding

Recognize the Limitations of Problem Finding

An Example Demonstrating the Attributes of Those Engaged in Problem Finding: General Electric

Summary

By now, the reader has acquired a working knowledge of the whole area of problem finding. Not only have the essentials of the problem-finding process been enumerated but several examples have been presented to show its application to corporate planning. Additionally, the last chapter stressed the use of decision support systems to assist in applying problem finding. In light of this background, it would be helpful at this juncture to discuss the attributes of an effective corporate planner when engaged in problem finding. This is the subject matter of this chapter. To complement this material, the next chapter will discuss common difficulties typically experienced by a corproate planner when using the problem-centered approach or the opportunity-centered approach.

AN OVERVIEW: RELATIONSHIP OF AN EFFECTIVE CORPORATE PLANNER TO PROBLEM FINDING

In the previous chapters, the accent was on the need to change one's thinking as a corporate planner for effective problem finding. More specifically, this centered on the need for greater objectivity; that is, the corporate planner must stand back and undertake an appropriate action for the area under study. In effect, an effective corporate planner must take off his or her "blinders" before trying to resolve the problems for specific parts of the organization. Otherwise, "the tail will be wagging the dog." To state this viewpoint in terms of the text's subject matter, the focus is on utilizing a problem-finding approach versus just a problem-solving approach although the attendant circumstances will dictate which one to use. From this perspective, an effective corporate planner must be aware of a number of desired attributes that the individual should acquire to reap the full benefits of problem finding. Due to their importance, these attributes are treated in some depth.

DESIRED ATTRIBUTES OF AN EFFECTIVE CORPORATE PLANNER ENGAGED IN PROBLEM FINDING

Desired attributes that a corporte planner should have when engaged in problem finding are related to those techniques found in Chapter 2. The problem-finding techniques—creative thinking, brainstorming, synectics, problem definition table, and checklists—provide a helpful frame of reference or starting point for a corporate planner. A corporate planner not only should be creative in his or her thinking process about corporate planning problems but should be open to new techniques to resolve future problems as well as identify future opportunities. For a corporate planner to be truly effective, he or she must change his or her way of viewing the world and the organization. How the individual views himself or herself should also change. In the material to follow, a number of attributes that an effective corporate planner should possess are explored. Although some of these attributes are self-evident, others may not be.

Take a Broad-Based View

First and foremost, an effective corporate planner should take a very broad view of future problems. The same can be said about exploring future opportunities. The importance of this perspective is that all important facets of the problem to be found will be uncovered. In turn, the proper approach can be applied to the problem's solution. If a problem is viewed too narrowly, a problem-solving approach may be used when, in fact, a problem-finding approach is more appropriate. For this first desired attribute, the corporate planner needs to take a broad-based view so that the problem is defined within its proper framework. As a result, the problem is developed such that a problem-centered approach can be employed. In a similar manner, if the accent is on identifying future opportunities, the opportunity-centered approach can be utilized.

Think Strategically and Analytically

For a corporate planner to be truly effective using a broad-based view, it is required that the individual think strategically, to integrate the factors that have strategic impact on the organization in the long run. This centers on relating corporate objective, corporate goals, and company strategies to critical strategic success factors. Although this discussion is the subject matter for a future chapter, it is sufficient to say that a proper integration among these factors necessitates the need to think analytically. In essence, there is need for a logical flow from corporate objectives that tie in with corporate goals which, in turn, are related to company strategies. There is then linkage to critical strategic success factors. Within this relationship, the corporate planner must think analytically about strategic matters of the organization. The net result is that there is a balance among these integrated factors (that is, objectives, goals, strategies, and critical strategic success factors).

Employ Feelings When Deemed Appropriate

Thinking strategically and analytically represents the facts and logic or the "real stuff" of effective problem finding. However, also important is strong emotion, sometimes referred to as the subjective feelings or "gut-level" feelings. These feelings can give the corporate planner the inner drive that is necessary to do an effective job of problem finding. However, when feelings become bias, clear thinking can go astray. A biased view can make the individual select facts that favor a certain point of view and ignore those that go against it. As some unknown wit put it more tersely: "Don't confuse me with the facts, my mind's already made up." Thus, in certain situations a corporate planner's feelings may be important and appropriate to the situation, especially when the problem being investigated is very poorly defined and involves a long time frame. However, in most situations, thinking strategically and analytically is the better way to go. The attendant circumstances will dictate the best approach for resolving future problems and identifying future opportunities.

Have the Courage to Be Oneself

The corporate planner should have the courage to be himself or herself. When the individual is about to make a decision involving future problems or opportunities, he or she can look to see which way the wind is blowing, can adopt someone else's choice, can check for a precedent, can do what others expect, or can do something else. But in the final analysis, it is a matter of being true to oneself. Psychologist Carl Rogers put his finger on it when he said, "I find I am more effective when I listen acceptantly to myself and can be myself." The message, then, is that a corporate planner should stand up and defend what he or she believes to be true.

Too often, all of the important information regarding future problems and opportunities have been properly assembled. However, the assembled information has been misunderstood by top management making the final decision because corporate planners have been too timid to speak up. In the end, the organization's best-laid plans will have been a waste of time.

Be Open to Growth

An effective corporate planner should express an openness to growth. "The potential in you is new in nature," said Dr. Ari Kiew of the Cornell Medical Center, "and no one but you can know what you can do, nor will you know until you have tried." A decision is the point at which the corporate planner faces the challenge of how his or her potential will be utilized. Although this potential is quite reachable within a problem-solving approach, it is even more so within a problem-finding approach. Thus, a corporate planner must be open to growing on the job by employing newer approaches to corporate planning, starting with the problem-finding techniques set forth in Chapter 2. This, in turn, is followed by being open and willing to learn and practice the problem-finding process.

Be Imaginative

Another desired attribute that an effective corporate planner should have is imagination. A group of children in London were asked, "What would it be like if people had two heads?" The question, designed to test original thinking produced some original answers: "You would be able to sing a duet in the bath" and "Everyone would see eye to eye with themselves." From a corporate planning perspective, how "original" is the individual's thinking? How often is it "borrowed?" Is the individual too settled in comfortable mental habits? Do corporate planners let the thoughts flow freely? Hence, imagination can often be an important part of effective problem finding. In some cases, however, imagination may well be the focal point of the problem-finding process where problems are poorly structured or where problems have long time frames.

Have the Capability to Fail

A typical corporate planner should have the "breathing space" that allows the individual the capability to fail. There is an ancient tale about a man who invented a stove. It did not work. But he discovered that it made a very good wine cooler in the summer. Failure can be a part of the learning process when using a problem-finding approach. "Life constantly yields us second chances," said author Lloyd Morris, "and it is grasping them that we put our previous failures to creative use." Since we learn by doing, we succeed only by having failed at some time. The effective corporate planner should expect to fail sometimes. However, the individual should build with the rocks that have been stumbled over. In other words, learn from your past mistakes. As the old saying goes: "The first time around is ignorance, but the second time is stupidity." In essence, corporate planners can expect to experience difficulties the first few times using problem finding. However, as experience is gained, the corporate planner will feel more comfortable and will have improved planning results.

Recognize the Importance of Hard Work

An eighth attribute deemed appropriate for a corporate planner is hard work. Thinking is not easy. Ralph Waldo Emerson called it "the hardest thing in the world to do." Working at problem finding consists of:

- separating real future problems from their symptoms;
- identifying real future opportunities versus assumed ones;
- separating the facts from fuzzy information;
- thinking through each problem or opportunity in order to avoid being trapped by fixed ideas;
- thinking in exact terms; not "They say . . .";
- considering events and people individually as well as avoiding easy labeling;
- looking at the nuances and avoiding either/or thinking.

To assist the typical corporate planner in everyday problem finding, this hard work should take into account one or more appropriate problem-finding techniques (refer to Chapter 2). In this manner, the corporate planner's work can be expedited and made somewhat easier.

Take a Flexible Approach

Another desired attribute is flexibility. Take, for example, Dr. Edward Jenner, when engaged in medical research. He studied case after case, trying—without success—to solve the problem of smallpox. Finally he shifted his attention from people who had smallpox to those who did not. He found that dairymaids apparently never were stricken. They caught a milder disease—cowpox. And it protected them from smallpox. This discovery led to the development of a vaccination and the defeat of a deadly disease. Dr. Jenner's change of tactics is an example of what Dr. Edward de Bono, an authority on resolving problems, calls "lateral thinking." To those who reach an impasse, Dr. de Bono recommends these questions:

- Is there any other way to express the problem?
- What random ideas come to mind when I relax and think about it?
- Can I turn the problem upside down?
- Can I shift the emphasis from one part to another?

The main point is that rigid thinking in corporate planning must be replaced by flexible thinking. Otherwise, problem finding probably will never be effectively implemented by a corporate planner.

Undertake Full Responsibility

Last, but not least, the tenth desired attribute centers on responsibility. When the Washington Park Senior Center in Milwaukee needed a replacement teacher for a writing course, Mrs. Catherine Otten was offered the job. She said that she did not feel qualified. "If you refuse," the director told her, "there will be no writing course this year." Mrs. Otten accepted the job. Why? "The words of St. Paul kept canceling every 'no' that I was determined to say," she explained. " 'Let each of you look not only to his own interests, but also to the interests of others.' " What is applicable to Mrs. Otten can also be applied to any corporate planner. Assume full responsibility for problem finding. Generally, failure to accept full responsibility means that the corporate planner is not confident in his or her planning results or the individual is not a qualified corporate planner.

OVERVIEW OF DESIRED ATTRIBUTES FOR AN EFFECTIVE CORPORATE PLANNER

Inasmuch as the typical corporate planner is concerned with making effective planning decisions on the job, the ten desired attributes described above are excellent prerequisites to effective problem finding. Essentially, these attributes are related directly to (a) analyzing facts in sufficient depth, seeing the important issues, and coming to a well-reasoned conclusion about future problems and related opportunities; (b) coming up with new ideas that have good pay-off possibilities for future opportunities; (c) finding new and better ways of doing things now rather than waiting for some time in the future; and (d) exercising good common sense and judgment as well as learning from experience to improve corporate planning skills. A summary of the ten desired attributes is found in Figure 4.1 Failure to understand and put them into practice may well result in less than optimal decision making for the organization's corporate plans not only today but also in the future.

Figure 4.1
Summary of the desired attributes of an effective corporate planner engaged in problem finding

1. **Take a broad-based view.** Allows the corporate planner to uncover all important facets of the problem to be found in the future and brought back to the present time for solution. A broad viewpoint is necessary for identifying future opportunities.

2. **Think strategically and analytically.** Centers on integrating the important factors that have strategic impact on the organization in the long run. Essentially, this involves analyzing critically the linkage of corporate objectives, corporate goals, and company strategies with critical strategic success factors.

3. **Employ feelings when deemed appropriate.** Recognizes that strong emotion—subjective feelings or "gut-level" feelings—may be appropriate for certain problem-finding situations.

4. **Have the courage to be oneself.** Centers on being true to oneself. The comments and opinions of others are important, but being true to oneself comes first.

5. **Be open to growth.** Utilizes new problem-finding techniques as a starting point to meet challenges faced daily by a corporate planner. In turn, employ the problem-finding process to solve future problems and explore future opportunities.

6. **Be imaginative.** Refers to the ability of the corporate planner to let thoughts fly freely. Imagination can be an important part of effective problem finding or can be the focal point, depending upon the problem or opportunity under investigation.

7. **Have the capability to fail.** Recognizes that success sometimes comes only after failing with previous attempts. As experience is gained, a corporate planner should experience improved planning results.

8. **Recognize the importance of hard work.** Centers on the necessity of thinking in exact terms versus general terms within a problem-finding framework. This recognizes the importance of utilizing problem-finding techniques to assist the corporate planner in undertaking his or her work.

9. **Take a flexible approach.** Recognizes that there are different ways of viewing the same future problems or future opportunities. Rigid thinking, then, must be avoided at all costs by a corporate planner.

10. **Undertake full responsibility.** Recognizes that the final decision belongs to the corporate planner. This centers on accepting full responsibility for specific action taken.

ASSESSING A CORPORATE PLANNER'S QUALIFICATIONS WHEN ENGAGED IN PROBLEM FINDING

Going beyond the desired attributes of an effective corporate planner, the question can be asked: "How effective are you as a corporate planner?" An effective corporate planner is not born but is made by being alert to acquiring problem-finding skills. These skills are internalized by the corporate planner over time, thereby becoming an integral part of one's personality in everyday dealings with organizational personnel whether they be in top management or elsewhere.

To determine if you are an effective corporate planner, the questions in Figure 4.2 are offered as a means of assessing your qualifications. If the reader answered many of these questions negatively, the subject matter of this book should be of great interest to you for improving your problem-finding skills. Even if you scored very well, there will be many helpful hints given throughout the remainder of the text to sharpen your skills. This will be particularly true when working with groups and the newer computerized management science models and decision support systems.

Recognize the Limitations of Problem Finding

Although the typical corporate planner should aspire to acquire this new expertise, there is need to consider the limitations of problem finding. A close look at any problem-finding situation includes questions like: "What are the restrictions placed on me by knowledge, time, energy, education, position, ability, and so on?" (Does the corporate planner have the required knowledge for the problem or opportunity under investigation? Is there sufficient time to undertake a thorough investigation?)

From an enlightened perspective, the corporate planner should make every effort to learn this new expertise and apply it where it logically fits. To employ a problem-finding approach where it does not fit results in a great disservice to the organization. Equally important is the fact that it sends negative signals to those in top management about the corporate planner's abilities.

Figure 4.2
**A list of questions to assess the reader's qualifications
as an effective corporate planner**

- Do you recognize the need for exploring potential problems now and in the future?
- Are you alert to signs pointing to the need to explore potential problems?
- Do you recognize the need for exploring profitable opportunities now and in the future?
- Are you alert to signs pointing to the need to explore profitable opportunities?
- Do you take time for sorting things out from the short run to the long run?
- Do you face difficult problems head on?
- Do you act rather than drift and "let things happen"?
- Do you keep an open mind to new opportunities and ideas?
- Do you keep up with small problems to avoid being overwhelmed by them?
- Do you set priorities in the corporate planning process?
- Do you review long-standing problems and opportunities to see if they are still valid?
- Do you do your own thinking or are you a chronic advice seeker?
- Do you try to have a backup plan on difficult problems?
- Do you take the time for careful consideration when needed?
- Can you sense when to make a quick decision?
- Do you face the fact that "the buck stops here"?
- Do you see a possible opportunity in every crisis?
- Do you recognize the need for new approaches to corporate planning?
- Do you employ newer corporate planning techniques to improve corporate plans?
- Do you integrate corporate goals and objectives with corporate plans?
- Do you integrate company strategies with its critical success factors?
- Do you utilize input from the various levels of management (top, middle, and lower)?
- Do you employ the newer approaches to problem solving as well as problem finding?

AN EXAMPLE DEMONSTRATING THE ATTRIBUTES OF THOSE ENGAGED IN PROBLEM FINDING: GENERAL ELECTRIC

For more than 100 years, General Electric has been a household name. It brought the world numerous inventions, from light bulbs to dishwashers to CAT scanners, thereby improving people's lives and creating many new jobs. In contrast, GE's most visible moves in this decade seem less exciting. In a cost-cutting campaign, Chairperson John F. Welch, Jr., has eliminated approximately 100,000 employees, more than one-quarter of its work force. In June 1986, Welch closed a deal to acquire RCA. In effect, Welch created a company that can outpace the economy and thrive even in the toughest of times.

Essentially, Welch changed General Electric's business. He sold $5.6 billion of "dogs," including Utah International (a mining company), and shifted resources from stodgy manufacturing businesses to fast-growing services and high technology. In just four years, he poured billions into an automation campaign that has produced some of America's best factories. Welch sorted GE's operations according to a simple criterion: to keep from being sold or shut down, each had to be number one or number two in its market. He then grouped the fifteen businesses that he said met the test into three "circles." They included services like GE Credit Corporation and a unit that maintains nuclear power plants; technology products in a high-growth markets like jet engines and plastics; and what Welch called the core businesses. These are the "big players" in such mature industries as light bulbs and electric motors.

Financially, the current numerical expressions of his management have been very impressive. Return on equity has been a high 19 percent, the overall profit margin has widened by almost two percentage points to over 10 percent, and profits have grown at a compound rate of 10 percent. The only poor year was 1985 when profits flattened. Since 1981, GE stock has risen more than twice as fast as the Standard & Poor's index of 400 industrial stocks. Adjusted for a two-for-one split in 1983, General Electric has gone from $30 a share to over $80. More recently, its price has gone over $100. From an overall standpoint, the corporation is in excellent financial shape. It is expected that it will continue this way for some time to come. In fact, it is anticipated that many of its businesses not only will continue to be number one or two in their respective industries but will be the most profitable ones in their respective industries. From this viewpoint, these businesses are considered to be GE's "cash cows"; that is, they are generating more than sufficient profits to pay high dividends. In fact, they are providing enough cash to allow General Electric to launch new business ventures. Hopefully, these new ventures will become important revenue and profit producers to enhance GE's future growth.

On the other hand, the current troublesome spot in the financial area has been revenues, which have barely moved upward. The slow growth impression comes largely from having sold off the losers. Sales of continuing operations have increased by 5 percent a year, above average for the Standard & Poor's 400. However, with the RCA acquisition, General Electric's annual revenues went from $28 billion to more than $40 billion. Welch can get profit growth by reworking RCA as he had GE. But streamlining is only part of a multifaceted strategy for keeping profits on the rise. Indeed, significantly less than half of GE's profit gains since 1981 came from rooting out waste and dropping unneeded workers. The balance flowed from nurturing the fast-growing, high-margin businesses, namely, jet engines, aerospace, plastics, and major appliances. They account for 40 percent of GE's revenues and profits. In Welch's tenure, those four plus financial services have shown annual earnings growth of 20 percent or more.

A Problem-Finding Approach by Operating Division Managers. Needless to say, Welch has not been able to accomplish this Herculean feat by himself. He moved authority for most decisions down to twenty operating division managers. Welch promoted a feeling of what he calls "ownership," urging operating division managers to act like entrepreneurs instead of hired help. This means letting these managers engage in problem finding where deemed necessary. Welch also promoted free communication whereby there was a feeling and a spirit of total openness—something alien to General Electric managers of many years ago who got ahead by knowing a little more than the employees who were below them.

A major part of Welch's strategy for improving return on equity and profits is using technology to leapfrog competitors. Using major appliances (or "majors" as the division is known within GE) as an example, in the late 1970s majors was stumbling, disorganized, and laying off thousands of workers in a painful industry slump. Today, the $3.5 billion-a-year operation has moved ahead, and not because demand is booming. Welch chose senior vice president Roger Schipke, a dishwasher marketing man, to turn majors around in 1982. Schipke looked at its future problems and related opportunities and brought them back to the present time for solution. Although the time frame to accomplish this feat took several years, the net result was that he cleaned house and automated the plants.

To illustrate what transpired using a problem-finding approach in the majors division and what continues to be going on, the following factors are taken into account. The first automated plant to go on-line was the dishwasher factory in Louisville in 1983. General Electric caught competitors napping; that is, it picked up twelve percentage points of market share with new designs that gave it advantages in both cost and quality. Currently, GE controls nearly half of the dishwasher market. The next leap will be in refrigerators. General Electric, already number one in the market, is about to beat competitors with a new line. The machines will incorporate unique rotary compressors that Schipke says will give GE a decisive competitive edge for at least three years. Besides being cheaper than the reciprocating compressors competitors use, the rotary versions are smaller— allowing consumers extra storage space. The payoff from such strategic moves is paying off handsomely for General Electric today. In a similar manner, the payoff is expected to be even greater in the 1990s. As mentioned previously, this "cash cow" is and will continue to be extremely helpful in producing needed revenue for new business ventures within either GE itself or its large RCA operation.

Attributes of Those Engaged in Problem Finding. Although the focus of the foregoing presentation was on the chairman and operating division managers, these top managers could not have accomplished this feat of turning General Electric around alone. It is obvious that they were assisted by a capable corporate planning staff at the home office and at the operating divisions. More specifically, their task was to assist in carrying out the mandate to remain competitive and profitable not only today but in the future. Under Welch's capable leadership, corporate planners and operating division managers were given full license to make changes that were long overdue. To a large degree, they looked into the future and determined what had to be accomplished to turn the corporation around.

SUMMARY

This chapter aimed at giving the reader an insight into the relationship between a corporate planner and problem finding. The main focus was on the desired attributes of an effective corporate planner. These attributes were explored in some depth along with determining whether or not the reader is good at problem finding. A major reason for exploring these attributes is that the process of effective corporate planning is concerned with employing a problem-finding approach. Problem finding was applied to General Electric. The accent was on exploring the role of those engaged in improving the corporation's profits—from the chairman on down to the corporate planning staff and the operating division managers.

5

Common Difficulties Facing a Corporate Planner Engaged in Problem Finding

ISSUES RAISED AND EXPLORED

- How can a macro approach help a corporate planner avoid the common difficulties when utilizing problem finding?
- What are the common difficulties that a typical corporate planner will experience when undertaking a problem-finding approach?
- How does practice make a problem-finding approach easier?
- How helpful could a problem-finding approach be to Merchants Cooperative Bank of Boston?

OUTLINE

Identification of Symptoms as Real Problems

Erroneous Information and Incorrect Assumptions

Nonuse of Appropriate Mathematical/Statistical Models

Rigid Thinking Results in Poor Solutions

Sensitivity Analysis Ignored

Insufficient Verification of Solutions

Lack of Control over Solutions

Overview of Common Difficulties Facing a Corporate Planner

Practice Makes a Problem-Finding Approach Easier

Lack of a Problem-Finding Approach to Pinpoint Critical Problems: Merchants Cooperative Bank of Boston

Summary

It has been said that a problem well defined is half solved. A problem can be defined as a deviation from a desired set of specific conditions or a range of acceptable conditions; these conditions are objectives (or standards) which are considered optimal. The difference between actual conditions and the desired ones can then be "a problem." The causes of a problem can be defined as those events that have or have not occurred or forces that by their presence or absence cause this difference to exist. Although these concepts are not difficult to understand, their usefulness in conceptualizing problems and developing solutions is enormous. Within the problem-finding process, a number of difficulties can be encountered by corporate planners. This is the subject matter of this chapter. Much of what will be said about the common difficulties or pitfalls in identifying future problems and related opportunities will be directed at the typical corporate planner's mode of operation.

BE PREPARED FOR DIFFICULTIES USING A PROBLEM-FINDING APPROACH

Although specific steps were enumerated in Chapter 2 for the problem-finding process, many times they are performed partially or not at all. Even if they are performed the way they should be, there is Murphy's law to consider: "If anything can go wrong, it will." Although everyday problem finding is not as bad as this pessimistic saying indicates, situations where every aspect of problem finding goes perfectly well are rare occasions. Hence, the corporate planner should be prepared for difficulties when undertaking this new direction in corporate planning. Before describing these difficulties, it would be helpful initially to look at the corporate planner who fails to perceive future problems. These same comments also apply to important opportunities of tomorrow.

Some corporate planners tend to personalize organizational

problems. Whether or not they are to blame, they often look upon organization problems of today and tomorrow as personal failings which are embarrassing. To protect their feelings of self-esteem, they rework the information received which suggests problems exist. In effect, their minds are closed to these problems. Also, they believe the information indicating that problems exist is not valid, or they ignore it altogether. In either case, the real problems facing the organization are never solved.

Sometimes, attitudes and beliefs can blind the corporate planner to an undesirable situation. For example, corporate planners in one company along with top management firmly believed that organization personnel in their company were lazy and were becoming increasingly so. When they were presented with evidence that a high rate of absenteeism existed, it only convinced them further of the correctness of their position. Even when an industrial engineer—using sound statistical measures in an analysis of daily attendance—proved that the high rate of absenteeism was caused by the change in work schedule from five days to six days per week, top management and the corporate planners still stuck to their initial analysis of the problem, dismissing the findings as nonsense.

The problem-finding process is too complex for the corporate planner to comprehend and implement. If future problems are extremely complex, they might not be perceived at all or they may be perceived incorrectly and defined in overly simplistic terms. Real future problems, then, are never solved due to the "blindness" of the corporate planner.

Many times, analyses of future problems and their causes are oversimplified by the corporate planner. The corporate planner will say, "It is a communication problem" or "a personality conflict" or "an organization problem." These are vague generalizations which are often inaccurate and so general that they cannot possibly lead to any kind of constructive solution.

Employ a Macro Approach as a Starting Point

A recurring theme throughout the text has been the need to take a macro, or broad-based, view in order to practice "management by perception" in an effective manner. By perceiving problems and opportunities before they occur, corporate planners can be *proactive*; that is, they resolve the future problem or opportunity on a current basis. This macro approach is extremely useful in anticipating future problems and opportunities facing corporate planners where the focus is on a long-range or medium-range time frame.

COMMON DIFFICULTIES FACING A CORPORATE PLANNER ENGAGED IN PROBLEM FINDING

It should be recognized that problematic conditions may operate within or outside the problem-finding process itself, thereby causing less than optimal decisions regarding the resolution of future problems and the determination of future opportunities. These difficulties can be caused in a number of ways. As examples, the problem evaluation phase is ignored, the wrong problems are identified, and the facts concerning the problem are incorrect. These difficulties and others can be related directly to the problem-finding process; they are discussed below from a pragmatic viewpoint.

Lack of Clearly Stated Corporate Planning Objectives

A common difficulty is the lack of clearly stated corporate planning objectives. Without one or more stated objectives, there can be a major obstacle to employing the problem-finding process properly. For example, a company without sales objectives cannot be said to have a problem even if sales are declining.

Since many future problems, particularly those with a long time frame, arise with which corporate planners have had no previous experience, there is a tendency to ignore stating explicit corporate planning objectives. When problems arise in unfamiliar situations, planners often are unable to tell whether or not there is a deviation from normalcy. Although they might sense something is wrong, they are unable to determine whether there is a problem or whether their discomfort is simply the result of operating in an unfamiliar situation. Confusion concerning the problem also leads to confusion concerning the corporate planning objectives.

Nonuse of Problem-Finding Techniques

Too often a corporate planner relies too much upon his or her past training and experience when employing problem finding. As such, the individual lives in the past and forgoes learning the newer methods and techniques that are widely available. The newer problem-finding techniques were discussed in Chapter 2, namely, creative thinking, brainstorming, synectics, problem definition table, and checklists. The underlying framework for these problem-finding techniques is "stretching"; the individual's talents need to be channeled in new directions which can add new dimensions to thinking about corporate planning problems and opportunities. As a result, the individual is able to look inside the problem or opportunity and "see what makes it tick." From this enlarged perspective, a corporate planner has new ways of viewing the inner workings of the problem or opportunity. This is not possible when the corporate planner adheres to a conservative approach.

Lack of Proper Employment of the Problem-Finding Process

The typical corporate planner may have clearly stated corporate planning objectives and may be knowledgeable about problem-finding techniques, but if he or she does not properly use them, the problem-finding process is worthless. The basic steps of the problem-centered approach (see Chapter 2) are generation, evaluation, validation, establishment of boundaries, solution, and implementation. Similarly, the basic steps for the opportunity-centered approach (see Chapter 2) are exploration, selection, examination of boundaries, solution, and implementation. Failure to follow these steps in a methodical manner will generally produce less than optimal results. If certain steps are intentionally or unintentionally left out or are performed superficially, the final outcome from using this corporate planning methodology will, for the most part, be less than desired. Logical-analytical thinking is necessary; it should be sufficiently rigorous so that future problems turn out to be opportunities in disguise.

Identification of Symptoms as Real Problems

When observing the facts, *symptoms* of future problems many times are identified as the *real* future problems. Obvious problems are often the symptoms of much deeper problems. Identification that fails to perceive the deeper, underlying causes often leads to incorrect solutions. In complex situations there may be many intertwined problems; some items are more obvious and stand out more than others. Corporate planners will fail in their identification process if they either identify only the most obvious deviations as the problem or identify only those to which they are most sensitive. To overcome this difficulty, an examination of all pertinent facts is essential during the initial phases of the problem-finding process.

Individuals, not the observed facts, are often identified as the source of a problem. As such, corporate planners look for someone to blame when a problem arises instead of trying to determine what went wrong and why. Identifying the culprit, however, in no way assures that the person who is to blame for causing the problem will not cause it again. This is because the underlying reasons for the personal failure have not been identified and corrected.

Erroneous Information and Incorrect Assumptions

When collecting and forecasting information, poor questions yielding useless or erroneous information often mislead a corporate planner. Questions raised in the initial phases of the problem-finding process are not carefully thought through and are asked without an understanding of why the information is sought. This information is often useless or out of context, making it misleading. However, once the right questions are asked, the answer to the problem is often found. The approach, then, is to ask the right questions. As an illustration, in a manufacturing plant, a product quality problem was detected over the last year. All kinds of reasons were offered and many solutions were attempted, but the problem remained. A consultant was called in and asked a number of probing questions. One included: "When did this problem begin?" A search was made and a date established. Next, the consultant asked, "What other changes occurred around here at the same time?" It was learned that a new piece of heavy machinery had been installed in the next building. Nobody figured that there could possibly be a connection, but a study later revealed that the new piece of equipment was causing enormous vibrations which, in turn, caused the machinery making the product to malfunction just enough to produce the quality problem. This example demonstrates the importance of asking the right questions at the right time in order to solve the problem.

From another viewpoint, it can happen that information is not received to signal that a problem exists. For example, a corporate planner may not receive feedback on his or her short-range corporate plans or may be told what the subordinates think the manager in charge wants to hear instead of what should be heard. They say, "Let's keep the boss happy and tell him everything is fine. If we tell him the truth, he'll blow his stack. Let's keep him in a good mood—at least a little longer." Hence, nonreceipt of pertinent information can be as damaging as the receipt of useless information.

It is necessary in problem-finding to make certain assumptions about the future. They can take the form of technical, standard, and planning assumptions (to be explored in Chapter 7). If the assumptions prove to be true in the future, the final decision based upon them should be relatively sound. On the other hand, if the assumptions prove to be false, the decision is most likely to be unsound.

The assumption that there is an effective solution to every problem is not valid. For many future problems, there are no solutions. For example, when considering future personnel plans, employees' needs on the job may not be able to be met to the fullest degree possible. However, creative efforts should be directed toward trying to fulfill those needs at least partially. Corporate planners should realize that sometimes there are no complete solutions.

Nonuse of Appropriate Mathematical/Statistical Models

Even though future problems and opportunities tend to be poorly structured, many times appropriate mathematical or statistical models can be used to assist in resolving them. To assist in their utilization, there are numerous ways in which a model can be simplified. One way is to ignore the uncertainty that surrounds the estimates of input data by using a single fixed value. Another way is to use a relatively simple mathematical relationship that may actually exist. Linear relationships are particularly popular, as opposed to complex nonlinear relationships, because of the great computational efficiency of linear mathematical programming procedures. Although the world is not really linear, frequently it is nearly enough linear within a restricted range of the decision variables that a corporate planner is willing to give up some accuracy in order to gain computational efficiency.

The scope and detail of a mathematical or statistical model govern the number of variables or items to be included in the representation. This, in turn, affects the complexity and computational requirements of the model. In order to make the model manageable, the corporate planner must normally deal (more or less independently) with small fragments of the total problem. It is also usually necessary to compress detail by dealing largely with aggregate variables.

Rigid Thinking Results in Poor Solutions

The main focus of corporate planning is on the development of accurate and useful short- to long-range plans for top management. Rigid thinking and the attitude that there is only one way to do things cause difficulties. Some corporate planners persist in using responses that may have been suitable in some previous situations but are no longer adequate to achieve corporate goals, to solve future problems, or to develop future opportunities. It is almost as if they believe that for a particular kind of problem or opportunity which arises, there is only one way to handle it even though circumstances have changed. These individuals are not flexible and cannot see that the old solution will not always work. When people persist in holding to their mistaken beliefs in the face of contrary information, they are guilty of *mumpsimus*. This word was coined in the Middle Ages when an illiterate monk persisted in using his "mumpsimus" instead of the Latin word *sumpsimus* (to take) even after he was told of his error and was asked to change.

Another reason for not selecting the optimal solution is that the solution is not checked against the problem definition, that is, as the problem was originally defined. Many costly errors occur because overly eager corporate planners are too quick to apply what they think is the answer before checking it against the problem as originally defined. When properly performed, problem definition usually entails several aspects. Although the solution agrees with most of the aspects of the definition, the solution must check out with *all* aspects of the definition. Corporate planners tend to be relatively anxious to do away with the problem faced. However, it is wise to think through the problem definition to see if the proposed solution makes sense. Even when it does, there is no guarantee that the solution is correct.

Sensitivity Analysis Ignored

Employing sensitivity analysis is invaluable to the corporate planner for answering a whole series of "what if" questions about solutions. In addition, it provides valuable information regarding the type of controls that are needed in each situation. If a solution, for example, is extremely sensitive to specific assumptions or variables, it would necessitate a very tight system of monitoring and control. On the other hand, if the solution is insensitive to the parameters of the problem, a relatively loose form of control is warranted. The degree of control as determined by sensitivity analysis is an integral part of the establishment of controls. Failure to employ sensitivity analysis from both viewpoints may result in less than optimal solutions both now and in the future. For instance, what impact does price have on profits and what if the product is a high-quality product as opposed to a low-quality product? The complexity of the business world requires that sensitivity analysis be an integral part of corporate planning for best results.

Insufficient Verification of Solutions

Verification of a solution is necessary to determine whether or not the solution is, in fact, still optimal. Verifying a solution only partly or not at all can result in less than optimal decisions continuing for long periods of time without the corporate planner being aware of it. Verification should be applied to all aspects of a solution. While only a small segment of the total populace (as defined in statistics) was used in developing alternative courses of action and selecting the optimal solution, conditions that fit a small segment may not apply to the total group. In addition, conditions may have changed which may well indicate at the verification stage that the solution is no longer optimal. It is highly recommended that verification be quite extensive to avoid "suboptimizing," that is, reaching less than the desired results. For example, the amount of advertising—an integral part of short-range marketing plans—to be placed in newspapers as opposed to magazines, radio, or television needs to be verified continually due to switching habits of the general populace from one medium to another. The time of year also can have a dramatic impact on the selection of the appropriate advertising medium.

Lack of Control over Solutions

The establishment of proper controls over the solution is often ignored by corporate planners. Many feel that the final step in problem finding is to select the solution for the future problem or opportunity, and that is that. The corporate planner's attitude is similar to that of a typical manager: "I'm going to do something. You won't catch me sitting around when there's a problem. I'll be out there making decisions." Perhaps this attitude is largely a rationalization for not thinking through the steps required to engage in problem finding.

The lack of establishing controls over the solution on a continuous basis may be caused by high costs. Costs associated with monitoring the solution may be greater than the potential benefits. If this is the case, the use of controls may not be necessary. However, most situations require establishing controls to ensure that the optimal solution reached during problem finding is still optimal. As an example, how large should the inventory level be for a newly introduced, fast-growing product? What may be adequate today may be inadequate tomorrow. Thus, there is need for strict control over the inventory level for products experiencing an increasing demand.

OVERVIEW OF COMMON DIFFICULTIES
FACING A CORPORATE PLANNER

Although the problem-finding process carries a positive connotation—that is, the corporate planner intends to take some prescribed action to remedy future problems and undertake profitable opportunities in the future—it should be recognized that every aspect of this process may not go perfectly as planned. There may be problems encountered by the typical corporate planner during the various stages of the problem-finding process. In view of this fact, the above discussion has centered on the major difficulties that are experienced by corporate planners. Where appropriate, possible remedies were offered to avoid these difficulties. Such an approach centers on the question of "What should I do tomorrow?" rather than on "How did I get where I am today?"

A summary of the foregoing difficulties facing a typical corporate planner is found in Figure 5.1. Although these difficulties were related to the problem-finding process, they are also applicable, to a large degree, to the problem-solving process (enumerated in Chapter 2). The attendant circumstances will dictate which process should be applied to the problems or opportunities under investigation.

PRACTICE MAKES A PROBLEM-FINDING
APPROACH EASIER

As with any new approach to improve corporate planning and the resulting operational performance of any organization, it is necessary "to crawl before you walk." The corporate planner should recognize that his or her first encounters with problem finding may not be as rewarding as the individual would like. However, by encountering common difficulties that are a part of problem finding and overcoming them one by one as more experience is gained results in an improved problem-finding approach to corporate planning. To try and make the first tries at problem finding "remarkable successes" is both unrealistic and does not speak well of the corporate planner. The very nature of problem finding does not lend itself to the "perfect practice" of

Figure 5.1
A summary of common difficulties facing a typical corporate planner when engaged in problem finding

1. **Lack of clearly stated corporate planning objectives.** Results in giving little or no direction to the entire problem-finding process.

2. **Nonuse of problem-finding techniques.** Centers on a corporate planner not "stretching" his or her talents to learn more about the newer techniques of problem finding.

3. **Lack of proper employment of the problem-finding process.** Refers to the misapplication or nonapplication of the steps of the problem-centered approach or the opportunity-centered approach for the area under study.

4. **Identification of symptoms as real problems.** Relates to the corporate planner encountering something or someone the individual considers to be the problem when it is only one aspect of the true problem.

5. **Erroneous information and incorrect assumptions.** Relates to asking poor questions yielding useless or erroneous information or leading to information that is not received signaling that a problem exists; centers on developing faulty assumptions concerning the future in the form of technical, standard, and planning assumptions.

6. **Nonuse of appropriate mathematical/statistical models.** Centers on nonapplication of appropriate mathematical and statistical models to assist in the problem-finding process.

7. **Rigid thinking results in poor solutions.** Focuses on the idea that there is only one way to solve a problem; causes difficulties in reaching an optimal solution.

8. **Sensitivity analysis ignored.** Centers on the corporate planner's failure to ask a series of "what if" questions about the final solution that could alter decision making now and in the future.

9. **Insufficient verification of solutions.** Refers to the failure to verify the solution for the total group versus a small segment of the group that was used in selecting the optimal solution.

10. **Lack of control over solutions.** Relates to the corporate planner focusing attention only on future problems and opportunities and ignoring control over present solutions on a continuing basis.

corporate planning. The corporate planner must recognize the multitude of difficulties related to poorly structured problems and opportunities that have a long time frame.

Realistically the corporate planner needs to sharpen his or her problem-finding skills over time to be really good at identifying future problems and bringing them back to the present time for solution. Similarly, a corporate planner must develop the capability to spot appropriate opportunities that are linked to these future problems.

The time period to become effective in this whole area of problem finding may be quite long. Typically, creative approaches take time and, to utilize them properly should not be rushed. Too often, there is the eternal push for quick results. In the area of problem finding, you get out of it what you put into it. A hurried approach generally results in mediocre results. The best approach to the problem-finding process is one that allows sufficient time for the creative processes of the corporate planner to come to bear on the future problem or opportunity under study.

LACK OF A PROBLEM-FINDING APPROACH TO PINPOINT CRITICAL PROBLEMS: MERCHANTS COOPERATIVE BANK OF BOSTON

To relate one of the common difficulties facing management and corporate planners, a case in point is the activity surrounding the Saddlebrook Corporation's Advanced System Project. Sixteen banks in the New England area have invested $14 million in a partnership set up by Saddlebrook (a Cambridge, Massachusetts, vendor of banking software) to develop a complex management information system. Although most banks have since written off their investments, the Merchants Cooperative Bank of Boston has remained committed to running the system some time in the near future.

Merchants is scheduled to move from its service bureau to the Saddlebrook system; it is prepared to run on-line for the first time with virtually all of the bank's customer transactions and accounting. Needless to say, it will be a "baptism of fire," because the bank plans to have no on-line backup. On the other hand, another bank that was initially involved in the project pulled its money out of the Saddlebrook partnership. The bank is the Andover, Massachusetts, Savings Bank which plans to stay with its service bureau. The following question may be asked: "What does Andover know that other bank officers may not know?" The answer lies in the fact that banks do not understand completely the tremendous amount of talent necessary to run an inhouse, on-line system. In a few words, the computer expertise required is much higher than most banks are willing to admit. While Andover recognizes this important point, the same cannot be said for Merchants.

The contrast in both outlooks highlights the confusion among midsize banks facing the challenge of computer automation. Fundamentally, these banks with assets in the range of $300 million to $1 billion are in an awkward position; they are too large to run their business effectively on conventional minicomputer-based packages, but they are too small to afford the capability to develop or purchase high-powered integrated packages, let alone the mainframes or computer expertise to run them. The end result is that most midsize banks depend on service bureaus specializing in banking, or on correspondent banks—essentially service bureaus run by large banks. However, service-bureau banking software tends to be outdated and inflexible because managers have to wait several months to receive custom reports on revenue and productivity analyses.

Going beyond these computerized problems, there tends to be a total lack of integration in service-bureau software, thereby preventing a bank from determining which of its home mortgage customers also have a savings account at the bank. This integration is deemed crucial to "relationship banking"—the strategy of identifying key customer and selling them new bank products, such as IRAs. With increased competition from newer modes of banking, it may be the most critical issue for remaining profitable in the years to come.

Need for a Problem-Finding Approach. In light of the many problems confronting midsize banks, a problem-finding approach by the Merchants Cooperative Bank of Boston would have initially centered on a brainstorming approach to determine the most important problems that should be addressed now. This approach would have identified erroneous information and incorrect assumptions about undertaking the conversion. Although management information systems are playing an increasingly important role in the banking industry, Merchants Cooperative Bank of Boston does not have the experienced managers to help them understand that role. Rather than acquiring the information technology expertise, the bank is throwing away millions on a system that it is in no position to evaluate, never mind use effectively when implemented. An examination of the problems confronting the bank are vast when evaluated and validated within their present boundaries. However, these problems are capable of solution by taking a broader approach to the boundaries of the problem-finding process—that is, including *all* midsize banks in the eastern part of the Untied States. By widening the boundaries to include many more midsize banks, they, collectively, have the resources to obtain a management information system that is needed. By employing a reputable software house to develop the desired system, all of the banks would benefit from the short run to the long run, especially to meet newer forms of competition in the banking industry.

Taking into account Merchants' need for state-of-the-art management information system technology as well as its desire to protect its investment in Saddlebrook, it would still seem hard to justify taking on a major system from a source whose financial soundness is far from assured, particularly when the system is untried and central to the Merchants' business. Although Saddlebrook is testing the system, running actual bank data supplied by Merchants' service bureau and then comparing that to the service bureau, it is generally accepted in the banking industry that *parallel processing* be extended into the post-installation environment with newly developed systems. Merchants is not intending to run parallel systems. When it switches to the Saddlebrook system, it will disconnect from the service bureau. Subtle bugs could conceivably wreak havoc before being detected. But more important, a catastrophic software failure might close the bank.

From a very broad perspective, these unfortunate possibilities can be avoided easily by employing a problem-finding approach properly. Similarly, there is need to avoid the common difficulties involved in the entire approach to problem finding. In this case, accent is placed on erroneous information and incorrect assumptions.

SUMMARY

As discussed in this chapter and previous ones, the problem-finding process carries a positive connotation; that is, the corporate planner is going to take some desired action to uncover and solve future problems and, at the same time, develop profitable opportunities for the organization to follow. However, in the process of doing so, the corporate planner should be aware of a number of common difficulties that can cause the best-laid plans to go astray. To avoid this from happening, he or she should study these common difficulties with the eye to avoid them. As stated at the end of the chapter, this can best be accomplished by putting the problem-finding process into practice; continuous practice over time makes it easier for the typical corporate planner. Equally important, the problem-finding process should be an integral part of the corporate planner's thinking process on a daily basis.

PART III

APPLICATION OF PROBLEM FINDING TO EFFECTIVE SHORT- TO LONG-RANGE CORPORATE PLANNING

6

Integration of Corporate Objectives, Goals, and Strategies with Critical Success Factors for Problem Finding

ISSUES RAISED AND EXPLORED

- What is a typical example of problem finding by a corporate planning staff?
- What is the rationale for clearly stated corporate objectives and goals when engaging in problem finding?
- Why should corporate planners concentrate on the development of critical success factors for their organizations?
- What is the linkage of corporate objectives, goals, and strategies with critical success factors for problem finding as found in the Grayson Manufacturing Company?

OUTLINE

Getting Started on a Problem-Finding Approach to Corporate Planning

Establishment of a Corporate Planning Staff

  Use of Problem Finding by Corporate Planning Staff

Need for Clearly Defined Corporate Objectives and Goals

  Relationship of Corporate Objectives and Goals to Corporate Strategies

As will be seen in the next three chapters, planning is the essence of management. When top managers plan, they look ahead, trying to anticipate growth, problems, and opportunities for expansion into new markets. Corporate planners also match the appropriate information resources to the chosen company objectives and goals along with the critical success factors. Due to the importance of these factors, this first chapter on the application of problem finding to effective corporate planning centers on their essentials. More specifically, it starts with an overview of getting started on problem finding, followed by the establishment of a corporate planning staff to utilize the problem-finding process. Next, a starting point for effective corporate planning is focused on clearly defined corporate objectives, goals, and strategies along with the need to define a company's critical success factors (CSFs). These materials are brought together by a discussion centering on the linkage of the foregoing items for problem finding by corporate planners. Finally, a real-world case study—Grayson Manufacturing Company—is presented to demonstrate this linkage.

GETTING STARTED ON A PROBLEM-FINDING APPROACH TO CORPORATE PLANNING

In order for corporate planning to be truly effective, a problem-finding approach is needed to provide the kind of information on which top management and corporate planners rely to perform their tasks when making important corporatewide decisions. Critical success factors are tied in with corporate goals and objectives and therefore play an important role in problem finding. This is the focus of this chapter. However, before explaining these matters, it would be helpful to look at the need for an effective planning staff.

ESTABLISHMENT OF A CORPORATE PLANNING STAFF

In order to develop effective corporate planning information for a typical company, a corporate planning staff should be created that is responsible for all corporate planning activities. This group should be free from day-to-day operations and should be charged with the responsibility of assisting the president and the executive vice-president. Included among their most important functions are:

- to establish new and challenging standards of performance that are in conformity with the company's goals, objectives, strategies, policies, programs, and procedures;
- to find future problems as a means to recommending opportunities for growth;
- to assure that growth plans on a one- to five-year basis are prepared;
- to assist the various business units of the company in the preparation of one- to five-year projections;
- to coordinate and monitor the preparation of a comprehensive plan for longer than five years;
- to analyze current and future operations with the purpose of improving them;
- to analyze business, economic, and social conditions bearing on existing or prospective areas of operations.

After top management has reviewed the work of the corporate planners, has evaluated the one- to five-year forecasts, and are convinced that the financial figures are reasonable and feasible, the composite documents thereby gathered constitute the corporate plan for the stated period of years ahead. Sometimes these "working papers" are regarded as company goals, objectives, and plans. In other cases, their significant elements are formalized into corporate goals and related to critical success factors whereby the various segments of the corporate plans for achievement are clearly spelled out in great detail.

Use of Problem Finding by Corporate Planning Staff

In view of their foregoing duties, corporate planners of a typical company must combine knowledge of today's external and internal environmental factors with a vision of the future. From this broad perspective, there is need to employ a problem-finding approach. More specifically, this refers to using the problem-centered approach or the opportunity-centered approach. The problem-centered approach can be best exemplified by starting with the corporation's markets. The president of the ABC Corporation, for example, recognizes that the future market for its electrical appliances may well change drastically over time. In fact, he is convinced that half of the eighty products being sold and manufactured today will not be sold five years hence. In view of this potential major upheaval in the marketplace, he has asked the corporate planning staff (consisting of three people) to get started immediately on this major area of concern.

As a starting point, the corporate planning staff formed a problem-finding group, consisting of the executive vice-president, the vice-president of marketing, four regional sales managers, and themselves. The group met for three days at corporate headquarters and initially centered on problem generation (the first step of the problem-centered approach set forth in Chapter 2) regarding future as well as present products. In effect, this group examined marketing problems by using a brainstorming approach. The major problem centered not so much on the products being marketed under good, average, and poor economic conditions but on the changing nature of customer buying habits. Due to the continuing trend toward smaller living quarters and smaller families, caused by inflationary times and other factors, the ABC Corporation is faced with developing new products to reflect the changes as they affect the home market. Additionally, the group brainstormed the trend toward more people living alone.

Based upon the information generated by the group, evaluation (second step) consisted of reviewing the marketing area of the future and its related problems. As it turned out, all of the foregoing areas were determined to be valid for managerial concern—the validation stage (third step). In effect, the continuing trend toward smaller living quarters presents a major problem for the corporation. In contrast, its present products are oriented toward medium- to large-size homes where space is ample to accommodate them. In view of this major problem and related ones, the group spent some time establishing boundaries (fourth step). Although the home market in foreign countries was considered to be a viable one, it was decided to channel the corporation's resources in the development of new products for the domestic home market.

Although a number of problems need to be solved, the major one was the first one solved. Its solution centered on developing a wide range of new products over the next five years where the products would be more compact and, at the same time, capable of performing a wide range of services to meet homeowner needs. With this new direction, the problem-finding group worked extensively with the market research group as well as with middle marketing management who would be in charge of selling the new line of home products. Overall, the problem-centered approach has resulted in identifying future product problems. In turn, these problems were brought back to the present time for solution. As a result, management by perception has been placed into practice by top management and corporate planners for determining future strategic marketing plans.

NEED FOR CLEARLY DEFINED CORPORATE OBJECTIVES AND GOALS

A starting point for undertaking the problem-finding process is the development of clearly defined corporate objectives. Essentially, a corporate objective is a statement of intent—what a company proposes to accomplish. It is a statement of what will be accomplished when it has been achieved successfully. Every company objective means an action toward a predetermined end. In establishing an objective, both the action to be used (how) and the object or end (what) to which the action is applied must be described. Thus, a corporate objective has two parts: a description of action and the object of the action. As an example, to be the lowest-cost producer in a certain market segment contains the action to be undertaken (lowest-cost producer) and the end (a specific market segment).

A statement of corporate objectives must indicate *measurable* characteristics. Otherwise it is impossible to determine whether or not the objectives have been achieved. From this perspective, there is need to set forth measurable goals in terms of a quantitative framework, including reference to a time frame. When clearly defined goals are lacking, it is impossible to evaluate the plan of action, and there is no sound basis for selecting appropriate people, materials, methods, etc. For example, a builder does not select the materials or specify a schedule for construction until the individual has the blueprints. Another example that relates to the previous corporate objective of being the lowest-cost producer in a certain market segment is one where corporate goals would include reducing total manufacturing cost by 12 percent next year and achieving a 20 percent return on investment. In essence, corporate planners will function "in a fog" until they know just what is to be achieved. In addition, an important reason for stating clearly mesurable goals is that corporate planners provide a means to evaluate their progress at any time and are able to organize their efforts into appropriate activities.

Relationship of Corporate Objectives and Goals to Corporate Strategies

Building upon the foregoing exposition, corporate objectives and goals need to be related to corporate strategies. In the next chapter, there is a discussion of strategic planning and its component parts. At this time, it is sufficient to say that corporate strategies center on the acquisition, use, and disposition of resources required to meet corporate goals. As an example tied in with the previous corporate objective (being the lowest-cost producer in a certain market segment), corporate strategies could include reviewing and upgrading all product standards—materials, labor, and overhead—as well as negotiating lower prices for raw materials and tightening control over yields in the manufacturing process.

NEED FOR CLEARLY STATED CRITICAL SUCCESS FACTORS (CSFs)

Experience with critical success factors (CSFs) suggests that they are highly effective in helping top management and corporate planners to define their significant information needs. Equally important, they have proved efficient in terms of the interview time needed (from three to six hours) to explain the method and to focus attention on information needs.[1] The actual CSF interviews are usually conducted in two or three separate sessions. In the first, the executive's goals and strategies are initially recorded and the CSFs that underlie them are discussed. The interrelationships of the CSFs and the goals and strategies are then reviewed for further clarification and for determination of which recorded CSFs should be combined, eliminated, or restated. An initial attempt to identify the measures is also taken in this first interview. In turn, the second session is used to review the results of the first, after the analyst has had a chance to think about them and to suggest "sharpening up" some factors. In addition, measures and possible reports are discussed in depth. Sometimes a third session is necessary to obtain final agreement on the CSF measures-and-reporting sequence. Overall, the CSF method focuses on individual managers and on each manager's current information needs. It provides for identifying managerial information needs in a clear and meaningful way. Moreover, it takes into consideration the fact that information needs will vary from manager to manager and that these needs will change with time for any particular manager.

Critical Success Factors Defined

For any business, critical success factors are the limited number of areas in which results, if they are satisfactory, will ensure successful competitive performance for a company. They are the few areas where things must go right if the company is to flourish. If results in these areas are not adequate, the company's efforts for the period will be less than desired. As a result, the critical success factors are the areas of activity that should receive constant and careful attention from management. The current status of performance in each area should be continually measured, and that information should be made available to higher levels of management.

As an example of critical success factors, supermarkets have four industry-based CSFs.[2] These are having the right product mix available in each local store, having the proper inventory on the shelves, having the products advertised effectively to induce shoppers to come into the store, and having the products priced correctly (since profit margins are low in this industry). Even though supermarkets must pay attention to many other things, these four areas represent the underpinnings of successful operation. In other examples, speed of delivery and quality of the product are critical factors if a small grinding-wheel producer is to compete effectively against larger producers. To a food processor, effective advertising and new products can spell success. For a maker of expensive dresses, styling and good distribution are what count. And a fuel-oil dealer must concentrate on assured delivery and competent furnace repair. Such CSFs evolve with the business, and they must be reevaluated periodically for their relevance to the company's stage of development as well as objectives, goals, and strategies.

In addition, critical success factors can be utilized at the organization unit levels. As with the foregoing approach, CSFs are those key areas in each business unit where "things must go right" if the company is to succeed. Performance of these CSFs is measurable and often brings to light the systems necessary to support the success of the business. Experience indicates that CSFs provide the common ground of communication between user and systems management vital for effective systems strategy.

Primary Sources of Critical Success Factors

From a broad viewpoint, the primary sources of critical success factors have been identified as follows:[3]

1. *The structure of a particular industry.* Each industry by its very nature has a set of CSFs that are determined by the characteristics of the industry itself.

2. *The competitive strategy, industry position, and geographic location.* For smaller organizations, within an industry that is dominated by

one or two large companies, the actions of the major companies will often produce new problems for the small companies. The competitive strategy for the latter means establishing a new market niche, getting out of a product line completely, or redistributing resources among various product lines.

3. *Environmental factors.* As the economy changes, as potential factors change, as the energy problem becomes more acute, and so on, critical success factors can change a company.

4. *Temporal factors.* Internal organization considerations often lead to temporal critical success factors. For example, inventory that is rarely a CSF for top management might become a high-level CSF if there is far too much or too little stock.

Although these four sources of identifying CSFs are determinable, critical success factors are different for an individual industry as well as for companies within that industry.

LINKAGE OF CORPORATE OBJECTIVES, GOALS, AND STRATEGIES WITH CRITICAL SUCCESS FACTORS FOR PROBLEM FINDING

A problem-finding approach, as indicated previously, involves linking a company's objectives, goals, and strategies to its critical success factors. From this view, top management and corporate planners place first things first; corporate objectives are defined first, followed by appropriate corporate goals and strategies that accomplish specific objectives. In turn, these are linked to CSFs which center on those areas that need attention. The identification of CSFs allows clear definition of the amount of information that must be collected to be useful within the framework of problem finding. This identification moves the company away from the trap of building its reporting primarily around the data that are relatively "easy to collect." It focuses attention on those data that might otherwise not be collected but are significant for successful problem finding. Additionally, CSFs can be temporary; they can be relevant to the present only or to the future only. Problem finding must be tied directly to corporate objectives, goals, and strategies along with CSFs.

Otherwise, the time and effort spent on problem finding that is related to non-CSFs will have very little impact on insuring the company's profitability.

Traits Needed by Corporate Planners for a Successful Linkage

Although the linkage of corporate objectives, goals, and strategies with critical success factors for effective corporate planning is required, it is not accomplished on its own. Obviously, this linkage must be backed and supported by top management. Management, in turn, must assign this task to corporate planners. For this linkage to be successful, corporate planners must possess a number of traits. These traits include:

- *having knowledge of the problem-finding approach.* This necessitates the capability of corporate planners to link corporate goals with critical success factors for successful problem finding.

- *performing careful analysis of each situation.* Corporate planners need to examine each situation to get at the facts, cause-and-effect relationships, and its strategic implications.

- *developing an appropriate strategy that fits the situation.* A strategy is necessary in order to develop and hold onto a sense of direction, purpose, and objectives. But a strategy is more than a choice of objectives; it involves determining what will be difficult, making an assessment of favorable and unfavorable factors, and recognizing strengths and weaknesses for a specific situation.

- *recognizing classical dilemmas.* There should be a recognition that certain future problems and dilemmas are not always unique; certain situations repeat themselves and nearly every manager faces at one time or another a common set of problems. Corporate planners need to develop competent judgment and an element of maturity that enable them to lift themselves beyond the bounds of their habitual responses and handle each situation appropriately.

- *using a variety of problem-finding techniques.* Typically, the range of future problems is so great that one habitual set of responses or choice of alternatives is entirely inadequate.

Although these traits can be incorporated into one's personality as a corporate planner, there is no guarantee that these traits will always bring success. However, failure to employ them may lead to less than optimal corporate planning.

CORPORATE PLANNING EXAMPLE—LINKAGE OF CORPORATE OBJECTIVES, GOALS, AND STRATEGIES WITH CSFs FOR PROBLEM FINDING: GRAYSON MANUFACTURING COMPANY

Grayson Manufacturing Company, a textile firm, has annual sales of about $500 milion. It manufactures towels, bath mats, drapes, and tablecloths. In addition, it sells cloth at intermediate stages in the production process. Production is handled at three cloth mills, a yarn mill, a dye house, and a finishing plant. This company clearly illustrates how effective use of the right information can provide a linkage between corporate objectives and critical success factors.

Relationship of Corporate Objectives, Goals, and Strategies to CSFs. Grayson's management reviewed the company's corporate strategic plans. To avoid competition from foreign imports, Grayson chose to focus on being the low-cost producer in the market niches selected. Inasmuch as Grayson values employee satisfaction as much as profitability, the company's mission was twofold: first, to be the dominant supplier of textile products to the most profitable segments of the domestic textile market, and, second, to provide a high-quality work life for its employees. Top management determined its corporate objectives to be: (1) compete in profitable markets, (2) operate as a low-cost producer, and (3) offer a high-quality work life.[4] In Figure 6.1, the first of these three objectives is broken down into the goals and strategies necessary to accomplish these corporate objectives. It should be noted that the corporation's goals are very specific and target dates are identified. For example, the corporate goal of identifying and entering five new market segments with high-profit potential next year is related directly to the corporate strategy of upgrading the market research function to identify high-profit potential market segments.

Next, the critical success factors were selected. Knowledge of the organization, coupled with a review of annual reports, helped the company's management understand what was strategically valuable to it. A series of interviews beginning with the president and proceeding down the organizational chart also helped determine the important strategic success factors. In a second set of interviews conducted from the bottom up, participants discussed the decisions and plans made to understand the success factors better—that is, the *strategic* success factors for the entire company and *operational* success factors formulated for each organizational level. In this way, those factors constant throughout the organization were identified. Typically, the more decentralized the company, the fewer strategic success factors apply to all units at all levels. In companies under centralized management, more strategic success factors are similar among different business units and executives.

As shown in Figure 6.1, the strategic success factors important to Grayson for achieving the first corporate objective included effective market intelligence, development of appropriate new products, and dominance in chosen market segment. For the second corporate objective (operate as a low-cost producer), the critical success factors were high labor productivity and low material cost. Once the CSFs were set forth, the next step was identifying the individuals to be motivated to achieve these factors. A network of people from various levels of the organization was identified for each strategic success factor. It should be noted that several executives in the hierarchy were not part of the network of critical individuals because they were not vital to achieving that particular strategic success factor. Finally, it was necessary to determine and communicate the key performance indicators, which had to be action-oriented, capable of monitoring performance, and acceptable to management. In contrast to the president who single-handedly selected the strategic CSFs, many people participated in determining and monitoring key performance indicators.

Relationship of Linkage to Problem Finding. The preceding linkage of corporate objectives, goals, and strategies to critical success factors is a prerequisite to problem finding for any com-

Figure 6.1
Relationship of corporate objectives, goals, and strategies
to critical strategic success factors for the first objective
of the Grayson Manufacturing Company—to compete in
profitable market segments

Corporate Objectives	Corporate Goals	Corporate Strategies	Critical Strategic Success Factors
Compete in profitable market segments	Identify and enter five new market segments with high profit potential next year	Upgrade market research function to identify high profit potential market segments	Effective market intelligence
	Increase market share 15 percent in high-profit market segments in which the company is the dominant supplier within two years	Develop a product line that fits the requirements and needs of the high-potential market	New products
		Expand product distribution network	Market segment dominance

pany, including the Grayson Manufacturing Company. It makes no sense for the company to engage in problem finding unless the overall framework is in place. The admonition of a few years back is appropriate here—"Don't sweat the small stuff!" In other words, do not waste time on small things, things that in the long run do not matter.

Based upon the linkage presented in Figure 6.1 for the first objective (to compete in profitable market segments), corporate planners at Grayson are well advised to go out into the future and examine market problems that are emerging. In this manner, the company can rectify potential problems today that may be disastrous to profits in the years to come. An integral part of this problem-finding process is identifying future market opportunities on which the company can capitalize such that it can beat competition. From this broad viewpoint of problem finding, the company's objective of competing in profitable market segments can be realized over the long run.

SUMMARY

The main thrust of the chapter has been on the development of an effective beginning for corporate planners when engaging in problem finding. Basically, this centers on the linkage of corporate objectives, goals, and strategies to critical success factors for undertaking problem finding. CSFs are those factors that determine success for a company or a business unit. These are the important tasks that must be done well to ensure success. As such, it is these areas of activity that should receive constant and careful attention from management. The current status of performance in each area should be continually measured, and that information should be made available to top management as well as corporate planners. In essence, the attainment of a company's goals necessitates good performance in these areas. It is, therefore, imperative that top management along with corporate planners receive constant feedback regarding them. In turn, this information is helpful for corporate planning—from the short run to the long run—in the form of strategic planning, tactical planning, and operational planning.

NOTES

1. John F. Rockart, "Chief Executives Define Their Own Data Needs," *Harvard Business Review*, March-April 1979, pp. 81-93.

2. Ibid., p. 86.

3. Ibid., pp. 86-87.

4. This example has been modified from Victor E. Millar, "Decision-Oriented Information," *Datamation*, January 1984, pp. 159-162.

7

Strategic Planning and Problem Finding

ISSUES RAISED AND EXPLORED

- What are the differences between strategic planning and long-range planning?
- What techniques for forecasting the future are helpful to corporate planners?
- What is the tie in of problem finding to a typical five-year strategic plan?
- How can problem finding be used by the Zale Corporation to improve strategic plan development?

Quantitative Techniques

Ways to Improve Forecasting

Development of a Five-Year Strategic Plan Centering on Problem Finding

Production Line and Distribution Planning

Technical and Facilities Planning

Financial Planning

Personnel Planning

Integration of a Five-Year Strategic Plan with Problem Finding

Strategic Planning Example of Problem Finding: Zale Corporation

Summary

In Chapter 6 the accent was on the linkage of corporate objectives, goals, and strategies to critical success factors as a way of getting started on problem finding. This chapter builds upon this material by centering on the development of strategic plans that are related to the problem-finding process. Techniques useful in forecasting the future are explored within a strategic planning environment; the development of a typical five-year strategic plan centering on problem finding is also explored. Such a plan centers on product lines and distribution, technical aspects and facilities, finances, and personnel. A strategic planning example that can be related to the opportunity-centered approach of the problem-finding process is also presented. A comparable approach is set forth for the Zale Corporation.

AN INTRODUCTION TO STRATEGIC PLANNING

Strategic planning has been examined from several perspectives in the business literature. As an example, strategic planning deals with what the organization is to be in the future. The time horizon is generally beyond one year, on up to five years hence and beyond (if deemed necessary). The policies that flow from strategic planning reflect an extended view of the organization's economic, political, and social environment; resource availabilities; markets, economics, and technologies; and other basic factors over a long-range planning horizon. For our purposes, strategic planning is the process of deciding the resources to be employed to attain organizational objectives and goals, as well as the specific strategies, programs, and policies that will govern the acquisition, use, and disposition of these resources. In addition, it is an integral part of the organization's functional areas. Typical functional examples of strategic planning are (a) research and development—investigation of long-range implications of pure or basic research and applied research in terms of potential new products; (b) marketing—evaluation of projected forecasts of new products and services as well as their relationship to new markets; (c) manufacturing—determination of optimal allocation of present manufacturing facilities as well as projecting future plant needs; (d) physical distribution—development of more efficient transportation methods from the company to the customers; and (e) finance—evaluation of long-term investments originating outside the company.

Strategic Planning versus Long-Range Planning

There are several differences between strategic planning and long-range planning. Strategic planning tends to focus on one aspect of the business at a time. Long-range planning, on the other hand, views the company as a whole. Strategic planning, because it focuses on one aspect of the business at a time, tends to be more structured than long-range planning. Strategic planning normally involves a few top executives, whereas long-range planning involves all managers; most important, strategic plans show expected results, whereas long-range corporate plans lead to expected results. Although these differences are of a substantive nature, many companies are using the two terms interchangeably.

Based upon these introductory comparisons, a broad-based corporate planning program starts with a realistic understanding of existing products, divisions, markets, profits, return on investment, cash flow, availability of capital, research and development capabilities, and skills and capacities of personnel, to name some of the more important ones. Analysis of present operations can be performed effectively by reviewing the past few years' performance as part of the evaluation of the current year's operating and capital budget forecasts. Significant aspects of current operations, evaluated in an orderly manner, are the basis for considering how well the goals and objectives are being met by the company. In like manner, explicit plans beyond the current year on up to five years, based on current operations and existing plans for improving operations, become an essential part of a sound corporate planning program.

A PROBLEM-FINDING APPROACH TO STRATEGIC PLANNING

Strategic planning involves the allocation of resources to programmed activities calculated to achieve a set of business goals in a competitive environment. Corporate planners look upon strategic planning as an instrument around which all other plan/control systems—budgeting, information, compensation, and organization—can be integrated. Hence, strategic planning is the vehicle available to corporate planners for solving the company's future problems, including the current ones.

From another viewpoint, most of the strategic planning information received by top management and corporate planners is by-product information originally generated for individuals in lower-level positions in the organization. They have received information based on someone asking the wrong question. "What else can we do with the information that we have already collected?" instead of "What information do you need at the top to manage the company?" and "What information do corporate planners really need to allow them to explore future problems and their related opportunities?"

To have an effective problem-finding approach to strategic planning, a number of factors need to be set in motion. Typical ones include the following.

- State that the problem-finding process is to be an integral part of strategic planning. The pressure to show short-term earnings-per-share gains is one of the biggest deterrents to having an effective problem-finding approach to strategic planning.

- Involve top management in problem finding. The chief executive officer has more influence on the strategic planning process than any other person. This individual can make or break a plan depending on the vibes he or she sends out.

- Get managers at the appropriate levels involved in problem finding. Too often managers are managers, corporate planners are corporate planners, and never the twain shall meet. The net result is that important input for problem finding is never forthcoming.

- Test the assumptions behind the problem-finding process. Corporate planners tend to depend too much on trade association forecasts, and the economists that trade associations hire tend to be too optimistic.

- Do not focus solely on short-range problem finding. The thing that makes strategic planning most difficult is the tendency toward everyday firefighting. In contrast, focus on finding future problems that need to be uncovered and solved today.
- Keep a balanced outlook. The point is not to overreact; when the business cycle is at its maximum rate of change it is probably the worst possible time to start making changes to strategic plans.
- Stay flexible in a problem-finding approach to strategic planning. Too often strategic plans are inflexible and involve too many numbers. Instead, utilize a problem-finding approach that looks at good, average, and worst-case scenarios.

DEVELOPING SCENARIOS OF THE FUTURE

As a part of strategic planning for either problem solving or problem finding, corporate planners should understand the rationale underlying the forecast being used and on what developments the forecast rests. In other words, they should know what potential developments could invalidate a forecast. As a result, corporate planners could systematically monitor particular developments and know what kinds of changes might occur, in what direction, and by what amount. Beyond that, they would be wise to think through in advance and select the actions to be taken in each contingency. No one should be taken by surprise because sales are either higher or lower than were forecast; there should be a plan for what to do when sales substantially exceed or fall short of the forecast. Hence, corporate planners should insist that forecasts be developed within the framework of appropriate future scenarios.

Briefly, a scenario is a sketch of what might happen in the future if a particular choice is made. Generally, scenarios can be classified as follows: (1) the *best* possible outcome that might occur, (2) the *most likely* outcome which is a mixture of good and bad sequences, and (3) the *worst* possible outcome. As an outcome of developing these scenarios, corporate planners become aware of the potential gains as well as risks that may not have been apparent before but, nevertheless, must be included in the analysis for effective decision making.

Developing future scenarios not only requires a certain amount of imagination and creativity but is very time consuming for those involved. Despite the time and talent requirements and related problems of coming up with accurate figures, estimates of the likelihood of events allow the corporate planner to develop future plans that focus on events that are most likely to happen. Similarly, if the worst possible outcome can be examined in some depth, contingency plans can be drawn up today for problems that are most likely to arise in the future. Generally, there is little need of contingency plans for the best possible outcome. The detailed analysis of the best possible, most likely, and worst possible outcomes, then, provide corporate planners with pertinent information that makes it easier to evaluate the leading alternatives and to work out appropriate implementation plans.

The practice of incorporating scenarios of the future into decision making relates to the management-by-perception principle. Fundamentally, corporate planners perceive important future trends and their impact on the company before they occur. They focus on the entire company as well as its parts, relating its continuing objectives to changing conditions. "What was appropriate for yesterday may not be proper today and in the future." A broader and longer-range viewpoint is necessary to perceive the future before it happens. To improve forthcoming organizational performance, quantitative or qualitative techniques should be employed to "get a handle" on the future.

Making Assumptions for Forecasts

An integral part of forecasted scenarios (that focus on three possible future states) is the inclusion of assumptions. Essentially, forecasting rests upon hypotheses—conditions assumed to be true or expected to occur in order to validate the forecast. A set of hypotheses, express or implied, constitutes the assumptions that support the forecast. Close examination reveals that a given set may comprise an extensive list of assumptions which may be classified as technical, standard, and planning.

Technical assumptions relate to the forecasting model. The choice of model is a matter of judgment that involves assumptions concerning the relevant variables and their interrelation. Different models applied to the same data can yield different forecasts. The same model may yield divergent results if different time spans are used. Naturally, the manager will hone forecasting procedures to obtain estimates with a reliability appropriate to the circumstances. In contrast, *standard* assumptions are vital to appraisal of the forecast yet merit explicit mention only by exception. Unless alerted to the contrary, the forecast properly assumes the continuing availability of normal sources of supply, reasonable stability of the tax environment, and so forth.

Planning assumptions relate basically to marketing, production, and finance strategies. The sales forecast is a *prediction* linking quantities to prices. Major variables controlling total sales and elasticity of demand lie beyond direct intervention of the enterprise and represent constraints on the forecasting process. Future financial data, as found in the budget, starts with sales projections. However, it is primarily an instrument of planning and control. Management establishes budget quotas to fix organizational goals, exert organizational control, and estimate the costs of over- or underestimation. Production strategies merit special comment. The bridge that leads from sales to net income in the budget is distinct from the external link of sales to the market. Sales forecasts initiate the design of a comprehensive operating plan, but management has considerable latitude in responding to the market environment. It may, for example, alter the product mix, adjust production schedules, modify inventory policies, or regulate discretionary expenditures. Consequently, any single project (or most probable) sale level can translate into a broad range of net income estimates.

Because the underlying events may each assume a variety of different outcomes and these may occur in diverse combinations, a large number of projections can result from very few assumptions. The complexity obscures the impact on estimated net income of changes in a single assumption and underscores the difficulty in deciding which assumptions merit publication. In view of this dilemma, it is wise to reduce the assumptions to the classification of scenarios set forth previously—namely, the best possible, the most likely, and the worst possible outcomes.

TECHNIQUES FOR FORECASTING THE FUTURE

Forecasting techniques of varying types have been developed in recent years to handle the increasing compexity of future uncertainty. Each has its own special use and, hence, care must be taken to select the proper technique(s) for a specific situation. The selection of a method depends on many factors: (1) the relevance and availability of historical data, (2) the context of the forecast, (3) the desired degree of accuracy, (4) the time period to be forecast, (5) the cost/benefit (or value) of the forecast, and (6) the time available for making the analysis. These factors must be weighed constantly and on a variety of levels. Generally, corporate planners should choose a technique that makes the best use of available data. However, when a company forecasts with reference to a specific product, it must consider the stage of the product's life cycle for which it is making the forecast. The availability of data and the possibility of establishing relationships between the factors depend directly on the maturity of products. Thus, the life-cycle stage is a prime determinant of the forecasting techniques to be employed.

Qualitative Techniques

Current forecasting techniques can be classified into two major categories: qualitative and quantitative. Qualitative techniques employ mainly human judgment to make future estimates and can be used when data are scarce, as in the introduction of a new product or service. Typical qualitative forecasting techniques include historical perspective, panel consensus, and Delphi method. *Historical perspective* assumes future forecasts will follow past patterns where several years of past data are required. *Panel consensus* utilizes the concept that several experts can determine a better forecast than one working alone. Data are presented openly to a group of experts to arrive at a consensus forecast. The *Delphi method* employs a sequence of questionnaires in which responses to one questionnaire are used to produce the next questionnaire. Data contained in the sequence of questionnaires are consolidated by a coordinator. The accent in these techniques is on hunch, intuition, judgment, and "gut" feelings about the future.

Quantitative Techniques

Quantitative techniques apply various statistical anlayses to data for predicting future events. As shown in Figure 7.1, they can be divided into four groups: times-series analysis, regression models, diffusion index, and econometric models. For the first category, *time-series analysis*—moving average, trend projection, and exponential smoothing—attempts to discover underlying trends and patterns from historical data. Based on the

Figure 7.1
Quantitative forecasting techniques commonly employed in planning and their data requirements

---

Time-series analysis

- *Moving average* utilizes an arithmetic or weighted average of a number of consecutive periods to forecast some future period(s). Generally, several years of historical data are needed for developing a forecast.

- *Trend projection* fits a trend to a mathematical equation and then projects it into the future by means of this equation. Data requirements vary with techniques used. However, several years of past data are required.

- *Exponential smoothing* allows for the inclusion of both the present forecast and actual results of the most recent period on a weighted basis to forecast future periods. Data on current forecast plus most recent sales data are required.

Regression models fit sales to economic, competitive, or internal factors by relating these factors via the least-squares method. Several years of data are required to obtain good results.

Diffusion index (based on economic indicators) relates a group of economic indicators—leading, coincident, and lagging—that are going up or down in terms of a percentage which becomes the index. Data on the forty leading, twenty-six coincident, and twelve lagging economic indicators are used.

Econometric models utilize a system of interdependent regression equations that relate certain economic indicators to the company's sales, profits, and so on. Data center on external economic factors and internal business factors.

---

analysis, the forecast extends the trend of the past into the future.

Another widely employed approach is the use of *regression models*. Such models determine the relationships, for example, of sales volume to various external and internal indicators that are thought to have a significant influence on it. In some cases, a single-equation regression model will suffice, while in other cases, a simultaneous-equation regression model will be needed for effective forecasting.

Another approach is the *diffusion index* which is based upon the leading, coincident, or lagging economic indicators. For each rising indicator at any point in time, a value of one is assigned. If some are stationary, they are counted as one-half each and added to those that are rising. A falling indicator has a value of zero. Their sum is expressed as a percentage of the total number for one type of indicator—leading, coincident, or lagging—never a mixture. The resulting value is called a diffusion index because it shows how widely diffused the movement of the various indicators is. Diffusion indexes above 50 percent usually occur during economic expansion cycles, whereas those below that level appear during business contractions.

A quantitative forecasting technique that has gained in prominence is the *econometric model*. Because economic indicators are available, forecasts for planning purposes can be improved by including economic factors in the model. For it to be operational, sufficient data must have been tested so that valid relationships between the company and the economic factors are established. Basically, an econometric model is a system of interdependent regression equations that describe the relationship of a company's sales or markets to specific economic indicators. Economic movement up or down, in turn, affects the level of business activity within the company. Thus, the corporate planning staff can relate the external environment to the internal environment in terms of predicting sales, profits, and so forth.

Ways to Improve Forecasting

While companies have made a substantial commitment to one or more of the forecasting techniques, they feel that the full promise of that investment is not yet being realized. This feeling is particularly strong among corporate planners, although many preparers of forecasts have similar feelings. The stumbling blocks to successful application of forecasting fall into the following categories:

- failure to plan a progressive set of actions to realize the company's full potential for forecasting. Many companies have made a substantial commitment to forecasting but fail to develop a progressive and effective plan of action for implementation of a forecasting program.
- lack of skills required for effective forecasting. A majority of companies, including many with a major commitment to forecasting, lack adequate user-preparer skills on such dimensions as providing forecasts in new situations, identifying forecasting opportunities, and selecting appropriate methods for new applications.
- disparity in user-preparer perceptions of the company's forecasting status and needs. The often substantial differences in perception of the preparers of forecasts and the users of forecasts hinder effective communication and focusing of a company's scarce forecasting resources on the most pressing needs.
- lack of effective communication between users and preparers. Problems of communication are cited repeatedly as explanations for past difficulties and as areas for focusing future efforts.

Knowledge of what problems are commonly found in forecasting can be a starting point for improving it. Companies that seem to be the most successful forecasters are characterized by an accurate assessment of their own forecasting status, careful matching of the forecasting organization to this status, assignment of essential tasks to users and preparers, and use of forecasting techniques suited to the stage of development.

DEVELOPMENT OF A FIVE-YEAR STRATEGIC PLAN CENTERING ON PROBLEM FINDING

For a typical company, a five-year strategic plan includes external and internal environmental factors. The internal factors, which are normally controllable by the company, are represented by the following components: (1) product line and distribution planning, (2) technical and facilities planning, (3) financial planning, and (4) personnel planning.

Product Line and Distribution Planning

Product line planning is aimed at expanding the present product lines and entering new product markets as well as expanding the present customer base by serving new market segments. In contrast, distribution planning centers on the increased use of selling outlets and/or other distribution techniques to sell the company's products, changes in pricing policy and pricing practices to effect higher sales, and consideration of new advertising media for more effective penetration of the company's markets. Both center on the long run for the company's marketing plan. From an overall viewpoint, they provide a starting point for initiating the five-year strategic plan that ties in with the other three components.

Technical and Facilities Planning

Technical planning is geared toward creating new or improved products both for established markets and for those markets in which the company does not participate or has such a small share as to be negligible. On the other hand, facilities planning is directed toward major facilities contemplated and improvements in processing efficiency at existing facilities. It also includes determining the percent of capacity that is now and will be employed with present facilities and machinery as well as the steps that are being undertaken to utilize excess capacity where available. After product line and distribution planning have been set into motion, technical and facilities planning is needed to determine how the products will be manufactured in the future. It makes no sense to engage in planning for marketing activities without giving consideration to the related manufacturing activities.

Financial Planning

Financial planning is directed toward projecting sales by product lines, gross profit (sales less manufacturing costs) by product lines, sales and general and administrative expenses, and net profit by product lines before federal income taxes. In addition, it includes fixed and working capital needs, return on investment by product lines, and comparable financial analyses and ratios. Essentially, financial planning brings together the other three components in terms of profits or losses by product lines of the future. It determines the feasibility or nonfeasibility of adding new products. Even though the company has the marketing, manufacturing, and personnel resources to enter new markets with changed or entirely new products, the bottom line is the determining factor for the five-year strategic plan.

Personnel Planning

Personnel planning centers on the projected requirements for company personnel. Included are key management personnel, white-collar workers, and blue-collar workers when considering turnover and future growth. Even though the prior three components are under control, this last component can make or break the best-laid five-year strategic plan. It behooves top management to give the highest priority to personnel planning, including important motivational and leadership considerations.

Integration of a Five-Year Strategic Plan with Problem Finding

In the development of the above components for a five-year strategic plan, company objectives, goals, strategies, and critical success factors were utilized. In turn, they need to be related to problem finding. More specifically, this means being able to examine the company's future problems and their related opportunities and relating their impact on the five-year strategic plan. If corporate planners put on their "blinders" in the search for future problems and the development of appropriate opportunities to overcome them, a company can be placed in an extremely disadvantageous position. Problem areas, such as the effects of inflation and high interest rates, need to be successfully balanced. Such corporations as General Motors, Siemens, and du Pont have done so in their long-term strategic plans. In addition, they appear to be successful in adjusting future strategies so that long-run profitability is reasonably assured.

Opportunity-Centered Approach to the Problem-Finding Pro-

cess. To illustrate the use of problem finding in the development of a five-year strategic plan, an opportunity-centered approach is used. The president and corporate planners of a company producing products for the home market are currently working with a group of outside consultants. Even though an extensive report was prepared and presented by them, the president and his corporate planners feel that something was lacking in the report. Fundamentally, the approach recommended bringing the company's product line up to date for the next five years. What the report did not contain were future opportunities to make the company into a "growth company"—an item of importance not only to the president but also to the board of directors.

Inasmuch as the consultants were familiar with the company's marketing direction, the president reengaged them to develop one or more new marketing directions that would result in increased sales on a significant basis over the next five years. Based upon this mandate, the same task force was reassembled for two days in an attempt to explore (step 1) new marketing opportunities that were not in the report but could be related to the problems uncovered previously. Using a brainstorming approach, opportunities identified centered on the company's critical success factors, namely, product mix, inventory turnover, cost control, and price. Referring to the first CSF, there was an extensive discussion on changing the product mix to include new products that would be built into a new home, condominium, or apartment. The net result was that significant space could be saved by taking this approach. Another opportunity identified included contacting appliance manufacturers and selling the company's products to them as promotional devices. Other opportunities centered on the use of computer chips to enhance their performance, use of solar heat to power them, and even the selling of the company to outside investors.

Upon conclusion of the exploratory phase, the task force determined (selected) that the entry into the home-building market (single- and multiple-family homes, condominiums, and apartments) offered a significant new opportunity for the company (step 2). Hence, the task force selected to pursue this opportunity. In reference to the boundaries that need to be examined (step 3), the task force decided to limit its new product entries to the domestic market initially.

To solve for the best approach to market the new products, the task force spent some time determining the appropriate channels of distribution to sell the new built-in wall units. It was finally determined that the present channels of distribution were inadequate and that new distribution channels would have to be found. In this manner, the company would be putting its "best foot forward" in contacting builders whose purchase patterns differ from the typical home, condominium, or apartment dweller. In summary, the opportunity-centered approach has identified a new opportunity today that would have been recognized eventually by one of its competitors tomorrow. Recognition today of a most important opportunity assures top management and the corporate planning staff that the company's resources are being utilized effectively in years to come.

STRATEGIC PLANNING EXAMPLE OF PROBLEM FINDING: ZALE CORPORATION

The Zale Corporation, a retailer of fine jewelry with over 1,500 outlets worldwide, has been using decision support system (DSS) software on microcomputers in its corporate development group and finds that it has improved productivity and accuracy in strategic planning work and capital expenditure evaluation.[1] The corporation also uses DSS on its computer mainframes. For strictly spreadsheet-type applications, it uses Lotus 1-2-3 at central headquarters and at the division level. Using Lotus 1-2-3 within a DSS operating mode, it is able to work much faster with a greater level of detail and look at more assumptions and options. In the past, this type of work was performed manually.

Among corporate development activities at Zale that involve long-term strategic planning are coordination of the annual plan (the budget), strategic plan development, evaluation of capital expenditures, forecasts of corporate financial performance, analysis of acquisitions, and store location and market evaluation. Many of these tasks require rapid turnaround to meet management's needs, and this necessitates immediate access to computer resources and report output. Some projects require special analyses by financial analysts. It was requirements such as these that led the group to use microcomputers and decision support software.

The corporate development group includes four financial analysts, a director of planning, and a manager of acquisitions who devote most of their time to planning and development. They currently use a variety of microcomputers with printers and are using the Micro DSS package from Comshare, Inc. They also have a system installed on the computer mainframes for work involving large amounts of data, such as the evaluation of capital expenditures. Additionally, each division has its own personal computers and prepares its own plan which is submitted to the group as a package of financial statements.

For the coming year budget, a special format is used. A financial model on a microcomputer summarizes the total corporation's results, based on the individual divisions' results. Each division fills out the statements and submits them on paper. With that, data are entered into the model and summarized for top management. Then budget review meetings are held where management looks at these individual budgets, and after initial agreement they are used to generate a summarized budget. Finally, the actual consolidated financial statements are developed which become the annual plans.

Use of Microcomputers within a DSS Environment for Strategic Plan Development. Zale Corporation's experience with the microcomputer DSS software has been very good. It is now able to prepare in-depth, sophisticated corporate earnings forecasts, acquisition valuations, capital expenditure evaluations, and budget summarizations. For the corporation's approach to strategic plan development, typically, the corporate development group sends questions, instructions, and required presentation formats to the divisions. When they come back, they are loaded into another set of models and summarized. With these models, assumptions can be changed—such as required debt and interest rates on the debt—and five-year forecasts are developed. These models are useful in telling what earnings would be and what changes should be made in buying to keep debt within certain levels. Inventory levels and markdowns would be adjusted to keep the debt within a certain limit.

Assumptions also are made regarding a new store appraisal. Capital among the divisions is allocated which, in turn, determines the number of new stores to open. The corporate development group runs the model a number of times, with varying assumptions such as "What if we allowed the divisions to open twenty stores that year?" or "What if we allowed only ten stores?" The model is run under each assumption. Based on the results, the approved strategic plan is determined for capital spending each year by the division.

An example of a recent project for which a microcomputer DSS was used is the formulation of a model to predict the financial performance of a new retail store concept. The model was based on many assumptions, all of which can be easily changed as various ideas are evaluated. Among the key model assumptions for twenty-eight departments were sales by merchandise department—percentage or dollars; selling space—percentage or square footage; back room space needed—percentage or square footage; gross margin—percentage or dollars; average price point; customer conversion ratio; customers per clerk per hour; average productivity; hours of store operation; occupancy costs; and salaries and wages by type of employee.

Examples of pro forma model reports that are produced with the aid of microcomputers and decision support system software include sales projection detail, five-year profit and loss projection, balance sheet, and discounted cash flow analysis. Also, DSS is used for determining store locations and for market evaluation, which is based on the demographic characteristics and buying patterns of that market.

Need for Problem Finding in Strategic Plan Development. Although the above approach to strategic plan development is better than the previous one, it can be improved upon by employing the problem-finding process. More specifically, this involves going beyond determining the number of stores to open in the future by answering such questions as "What future problems can be expected in the opening of these stores?" and "What impact will these problems have on the company's critical success factors, not to mention company profits and return on investment?" All in all, problem finding has the capability of viewing strategic plan development from a three-dimensional perspective, allowing an understanding of what will make the new store "tick" in terms of future problems and related new opportunities not found currently in the corporation's present stores. This new direction in viewing strategic plan development will give the corporation a better view of its future so as to employ its resources in an optimal manner.

SUMMARY

As indicated throughout the chapter, the necessity for strategic planning lies in the fact that serious mistakes can be made if managers do not take the proper direction. A strategic plan is a company's map for the future. It is a way of looking at the company's weaknesses, opportunities, threats, and strengths so corporate planners can determine how to exploit or avoid them. In effect, a typical five-year strategic plan requires a thorough knowledge of the business, an understanding of the organization—both its development and its philosophy—and an appreciation of the capabilities of technology. When corporate planners go through the process of strategic planning, they acquire an understanding of the company's business objectives and the role each operational area plays in achieving those objectives. Only then can they effectively determine the resources needed and how best to obtain them. However, in order to take the accomplishment of corporate objectives one step further, corporate planners need to employ problem finding in order to integrate into the strategic plan solutions to future problems and their related opportunities.

NOTE

1. William C. Lewis, "Corporate Development with DSS," *Micro Manager*, November 1984, p. 10.

8

Tactical Planning and Problem Finding

ISSUES RAISED AND EXPLORED

- What are the principal differences between tactical planning and medium-range planning?
- What techniques are useful in reducing uncertainty and risk to managers as well as corporate planners?
- What is the linkage of problem finding to a typical tactical plan for the coming year?
- How can problem finding be useful to the Phillips Petroleum Company in reaching its corporate objectives?

Decision Trees

Risk Analysis

Development of Coming Year Tactical Plan Centering on Problem Finding

Essential Components of the Tactical Plan

Integration of the Coming Year Tactical Plan with Problem Finding

Tactical Planning Example of Problem Finding: Phillips Petroleum Company

Summary

The material of this chapter is linked with the prior one; that is, a comprehensive strategic plan provides input for a more detailed tactical plan for the coming year. In turn, a tactical plan provides the needed input for a very detailed operational plan examined in the next chapter. As a starting point, this chapter distinguishes between tactical planning and medium-range planning, followed by a problem-finding approach to the chapter's subject matter. After discussing the techniques for reducing uncertainty and risk, the development of a typical tactical plan for the coming year is set forth along with an example of an opportunity-centered approach to problem finding. Finally, the need for problem finding at the middle-management level is explored for the Phillips Petroleum Company.

AN INTRODUCTION TO TACTICAL PLANNING

Tactical planning is a continuation of strategic planning and the interface with operational planning. While strategic planning has been undertaken by top management and corporate planners, tactical planning is the job of middle management. As discussed in the last chapter, strategic planning is a way of looking at the large picture. It considers future trends as well as present business objectives. It answers why we are in business and where we are headed. With strategic planning, managers try to set broad organizational directives and establish priorities. They identify the direction to be followed.

Tactical planning, however, concerns itself with the methods and tools needed to achieve the strategic objectives. It answers how we get where we plan to go. It is the tactical areas that receive the objectives of corporate planners and begin to assemble the resources required and make decisions about priorities in allocating those resources. As such, tactical planning is a continuation of strategic planning at the middle-management levels.

Tactical Planning versus Medium-Range Planning

Tactical planning deals with the physical implementation of the company's long-range strategic plans. It includes capital budgeting, the coming year budget, facility expansion or shutdown, price setting, product line, and market development decisions. Tactical planning often is concerned primarily with future facilities or product planning, and the time horizon is related to the lead time for new major facilities in the particular system. The time horizon can be one year and, at times, can be much longer. An example of tactical planning is determining the size, location, cost, and technology of new refinery processing units needed to meet forecast changes in crude oil availability and refined product requirements for the next three years.

Medium-range planning, which centers around the second-year planning period, is a subset of long-range corporate planning. For example, a five-year corporate plan that involves product line, marketing, technical, facilities and production, personnel, and financial planning is stated in more detail for this level. Essentially, the accent is on developing important budgets for the following year, that is, the second year. First, the areas of marketing and manufacturing are detailed before appropriate budgets are determined for selling, material purchases, labor, manufacturing overhead, and general and administrative expenses. All the income and expense factors are expressed in terms of a cash budget. Finally, the results of the preceding budgets are expressed in a projected balance sheet and an income statement with supporting schedules and sources and applications of funds. It should be noted that throughout the budgeting analysis phase, certain constraints can be integrated into the budgeting process if and when deemed necessary by corporate planners.

The budgeting process for tactical planning or medium-range planning has several important aspects when performed with the help of a computer system. First, certain assumptions as to what will happen can be tested by "passing" the transactions representing these assumptions through the budget system. Second, the computer can perceive what the financial effects of actions will be, whether they are favorable or unfavorable. Third, the computer can determine whether or not some condition or constraint has been violated—for example, if working capital availability in the future has been violated. In essence, an effective computer approach to budgeting permits the company to respond to the dynamics of the situation. It allows changes to budgets whenever something significant happens to alter conditions.

A PROBLEM-FINDING APPROACH
TO TACTICAL PLANNING

The questions asked within a strategic planning environment can also be asked for tactical planning. However, the difference is that these broad, overview questions become more specific. For example, "What corporate planning information is needed by top management and corporate planners to give direction to the company tomorrow?" needs to be changed to "What tactical plans are needed by middle-level managers to insure a high-level of sales (say increasing by 15% per year) and profitability (say 20% on each sales dollar) for the coming year?" To assist in reaching these goals of these tactical plans, a problem-finding approach is extremely helpful to middle management which is working with corporate planners. As a means of assisting in the problem-finding approach—especially in improving a company's opportunity for improved profitability—a budget simulation model or a fourth-generation financial planning language can be used by corporate planners. Each is explored briefly below.

Budget Simulation Model

In this first approach, a budget simulation model brings into play strategic budgeting data with the latest income and expense data elements. Output from the budget program is selected financial information: in particular, income statement, balance sheet, cash flow, and source and application of funds for the coming year. A CRT terminal can be utilized to simulate the data to answer "what if" questions for assistance in problem finding, to store new information, or to change existing data.

In developing a corporate budget model, the existing budgeting system must be an excellent analogue or a measurable simulation of the company. Its output mirrors the company's physical activities. Of course, it should be recognized that some differences are inevitable between the actual accounting/budgeting system and any model of it. One of these is the way in which the values of system variables (accounts) are derived. The actual system interacts with external parties and then processes these transactions by changing the balances in the appropriate accounts. In contrast, a simulation model does not have real transactions to make changes in the balances of various accounts. The user of such a model must create artificial transactions which have a high degree of similarity to the expected real-life version. The manner of processing these transactions, then, is by formulating equations that define the value of the various accounts.

Another factor in constructing the model is to make sure that it is valid. It must be a good approximation of reality. Here experience and intuition are indispensable. Seasoned judgment is the only way to decide finally whether or not the output of the model is reliable. Subtle relationships are discovered and new insights about the operation of the company are learned.

Financial Planning Language

Although the budget simulation model can be used by corporate planners, they may prefer to work with a simple-to-use financial planning language, such as the Interactive Financial Planning System (IFPS) (a fourth-generation language). For applications such as projected financial statements next year or several years in the future, corporate cash flow, and deciding whether to float a bond issue or sell additional stock, corporate planners have used this planning language with good results. Similarly, they have used IFPS for leasing plans versus purchasing over the next several years, as well as for merger/acquisition analysis. All in all, IFPS has been used successfully due to its simplicity and timeliness and because it allows corporate planners interfacing with it to have full control.

TECHNIQUES FOR REDUCING UNCERTAINTY
AND RISK

Currently, there are a number of techniques to assist in tactical planning for reducing uncertainty and risk. Some of the more popular ones for exploring best possible, most likely, and worst possible outcomes are (1) decision theory, (2) decision trees, and (3) risk analysis. It should be noted that a range of values can be developed using these techniques in place of the three outcomes. Each of these techniques for reducing future uncertainty is explored below.

Decision Theory

Decision theory is quite useful in reducing the uncertainty factor; it can be segregated into decision making under certainty, risk, and uncertainty. Decision making under certainty (first approach) is highly desirable since all relevant factors are known with complete certainty. The probability that the event will occur is either zero or one; the decision maker knows that the event will occur or will not occur. Thus, under conditions of certainty, decision making is straightforward since the most profitable project alternative is selected. However, this approach is rarely applicable to future events since one is not able to predict the future with absolute certainty.

In using decision theory under conditions of risk (second approach), one can look upon risk as measurable uncertainty. In a risk situation, the outcome is uncertain, but the results of previous experience are available and can be used to determine the probability that the outcome will occur again. Probabilities associated with risk range from "greater than zero" to "less than one." If past or objective probabilities cannot be determined, the decision maker must estimate subjectively the chances of occurrence of the outcome under certain assumptions. This procedure converts a risk situation to an uncertainty condition (third approach). Therefore, whenever subjective probabilities are utilized in an analysis, the decision maker is reducing the degree of uncertainty for future projections.

Certainty and uncertainty can be thought of as the extremes

of the decision theory continuum. This is not to say that certainty stipulates what will happen and that uncertainty denotes what will not happen. Rather, certainty operates in a known environment, while uncertainty operates in an unknown environment where the chances that an outcome will occur are not always completely predictable. (Chance is used here as synonymous with probability.)

Decision theory has been widely employed by business planners over the years. Some of the first corporations to use it include du Pont, Pillsbury Company, General Electric Company, General Mills, Inmont Corporation, Ford Motor Company, and Time. Today, there is a whole host of companies that have adopted this approach.

Decision Trees

A decision tree offers an added dimension to decision-making skills, since it factors the degree of uncertainty or the probability of future occurrences into a decision. This simple mathematical tool enables the decision maker to consider various courses of action under certain assumptions, assign financial results to them, modify these results by their probability, and make comparisons. It is so called because it looks like a tree, although for the sake of convenience, it is depicted horizontally. The base of the tree is the present decision point, usually represented graphically by a small square. Its branches began at the first chance event (represented by a circle). Each chance event produces two or more possible events, some of which lead to other chance events and subsequent decision points. Information on which the tree's values are based is derived from careful research, which provides probabilities that certain chance events will occur and predicted payout or cash flow estimates for each possible outcome, as influenced by various possible chance events.

Basically, the technique provides a comparatively simple graphic method for analyzing the potential outcomes of a complex decision. It offers a way of showing the interplay between a present decision, chance events, and possible future decisions, as well as enables the evaluation of the available opportunities. The highest value indicates the course most likely to produce the greatest return for the company. To solve the problem, the concept of rollback must be employed. To roll back the tree, one begins at the right-hand terminus of the tree and works back to the current decision point. Most planning decisions require trees with numerous branches and more than one decision pont. It is the multiplicity of decision points that makes the rollback process necessary.

Risk Analysis

Risk analysis can be viewed from two different perspectives. From one perspective, the aim is to eliminate risk, or, at least, to minimize it. From another perspective, risk analysis is designed to make the company capable of taking not only bigger risks, but the right ones. Regardless of the perspective used, risk analysis recognizes that important company decisions are made in the face of incomplete information.

Managers have long spoken of "running a calculated risk," but it is now possible to calculate risks in tactical planning decisions. This development holds both the impetus and the means for more effective relations between the managers who must make actual decisions and the staff which produces advice on how decisions ought to be made. In particular, it appears possible that analyses involving risk will give staff advisers considerably greater insight into the processes of decision making, which managers use so well but talk about so vaguely.

Techniques, such as payback and rate of return analysis, have been developed to quantify the capital investment decision. However, most of these computational methods do not take into account the statistical nature of investment decisions—the "riskiness" of a future outcome. Computer programs are available that use simulation techniques to evaluate investment decisions by analyzing the risk involved. They impose almost no restrictions on the situation being studied and can be understood with a little effort. Although these risk analysis programs cannot predict an outcome exactly, they do offer a rational procedure that can be used by a decision maker to select the most profitable investments. A typical risk analysis program is General Risk Analysis Simulation Package (GRASP). GRASP was developed by the Gulf Oil Company and West Virginia University in order to provide Gulf management with techniques for investment planning and to promote the use of risk simulation packages.

A summary of the above techniques for reducing uncertainty and risk is set forth in Figure 8.1.

Figure 8.1
A summary of typical techniques for reducing uncertainty and risk within a corporate planning environment

---

Decision theory. Useful in reducing the uncertainty factor in planning decisions by applying probability factors that assess the likelihood of the occurrences of a planned event.

Decision trees. Graphical representations of possible actions and events utilizing probability factors which allow the planner to trace the optimal path through a tree diagram.

Risk analysis. Recognizes that planning decisions are made in face of incomplete information which can be overcome to a certain degree by subjecting risks in business planning to simulation procedures.

DEVELOPMENT OF COMING YEAR TACTICAL PLAN CENTERING ON PROBLEM FINDING

Development of a tactical plan for a typical company is related to a five-year strategic plan (see Chapter 7). However, the time frame is reduced considerably; typically it is for the next year. This time frame was illustrated above for the computerized budgeting approach. Generally, a company uses tactical planning on a regular basis to determine yearly profit targets for each business unit as a function of projected demand for various products. The tactical planning system should be flexible so that corporate planners can adjust annual plans every quarter as near-term demand projections become definite. The major features of the resulting plans can then be displayed as a set of mutually consistent subplans for procurement, production, and transportation. In turn, the implications of each of these plans can be further detailed by surrounding systems.

Essential Components of the Tactical Plan

A tactical plan, like a five-year strategic plan, includes the same components. By way of review, they are product line and distribution planning, technical and facilities planning, financial planning, and personnel planning. Although the focus has been on the third component, the first component will be related to problem finding below.

Integration of the Coming Year Tactical Plan with Problem Finding

As with strategic planning, it is necessary to relate corporate objectives, goals, strategies, and critical success factors to problem finding for tactical planning. This linkage can be best illustrated by referring to the first component discussed above, namely, product line and distribution planning. In order to facilitate this component, reference can be made to a typical corporation that has an objective to expand its sales in profitable markets. This means setting a goal of identifying new customers and/or market segments that have high sales potential for the coming year. To accomplish this goal an opportunity-centered approach is necessary. Essentially, the focus could be directed toward customer credit information, thereby signaling new marketing opportunities.

Opportunity-Centered Approach to the Problem-Finding Process. Utilizing the opportunity-centered approach, exploration (step 1) relates to searching the environment for opportunities that come from problems uncovered. This initial step is undertaken by a problem-finding group. Essentially, the focus is on identifying potential customers who buy large quantities and who have a good credit rating. In addition, it means searching for those customers who may have need of specialized products for the markets they serve. Not only large customers represent potential opportunities for expanding the corporation's sales volume; small- and medium-size companies also represent ways of expanding corporation sales.

Based upon the foregoing opportunities, the selection process (step 2) centers on determining that one or more opportunities should be explored by management. After a lengthy discussion, the group finally resolved which of the above opportunities should be explored initially. Because the corporation has approximately 30 percent excess production capacity currently, it was decided that past and current medium-sized companies should be the target for obtaining credit information along with specific sales proposals to entice them to buy from the corporation. Within the selection process, the boundaries were examined (step 3) in terms of available factory capacity.

The solution to the foregoing opportunity to promote prospective medium-sized customers rather than wait for them to come to the corporation resulted in the need for the credit and collection section to make some calculations. This section needs to supply the marketing department with specific sales amounts that can be ordered by prospective customers. This can be determined quite easily with a computerized approach. Thus, the marketing department can send special promotion letters that are backed by salesperson calls to past and current medium-size companies. In this manner, there is no need for going through the credit process which, many times, results in asking the customer to reduce the order size due to credit rating problems. In essence, the corporation is putting its best foot forward by specifying the sales amount that it will accept without question. Overall, the opportunity-centered approach in the credit and collection section has taken a positive approach to promoting new customers.

TACTICAL PLANNING EXAMPLE OF PROBLEM FINDING: PHILLIPS PETROLEUM COMPANY

To illustrate tactical planning in marketing as well as other functional areas, the Phillips Petroleum Company has recently implemented a decision support system (DSS) designed for use by middle management in need of an efficient method of integrating problem solving.[1] As described below, microcomputers and computer mainframes are used to make management users responsible for decision support system applications. These applications include not only marketing but areas related to marketing, such as budget planning and production. To ensure overall DSS effectiveness and to aid users, an extensive support framework has been instituted which includes user computing services, operations research (management science), data-processing operations, and distributed data processing. This integration of marketing with other functional areas represents the current direction of DSS using microcomputers and similar types of equipment.

Use of Computers within a DSS Environment for Tactical Marketing Applications. The Phillips Petroleum Company has implemented an extensive program of software acquisition, training, and support to make management "user responsible" for decision support system applications. Through DSS, the functions of the operating groups of Phillips which include Minerals, Exploration and Production, Gas and Gas Liquids, Corporate, Petroleum Products, and Chemicals are woven together. They can work autonomously or interchangeably through DSS. The approach is based upon the broad concept that decision support systems are computer-based systems that help decision makers, such as middle management and group leaders, utilize data and models to solve unstructured problems, such as forecasting and tactical marketing applications. Placing DSS responsibility in management's hands is an efficient means of generating these views of the business (reports), which depend on continually redefined data, such as market changes and economic variables.

Phillips had formerly handled DSS in more traditional ways. Data-processing groups generated decision support reports based on criteria given by management or operating teams. This was a time-consuming process. However, new software packages that are no longer programming-oriented but user-oriented "fourth-generation languages" enable the decision makers to generate these reports themselves, as needed. The net result is that DSS allows the company to get out of the software development business and puts the user into it, without sacrificing the power to develop complex applications. In some cases, the user can be taught in only one day to create an application program, with a user-friendly interface developed by a programmer-analyst, offering full-screen, scrolling, and system-edited reports with color graphics.

In addition to the marketing applications for assisting middle management, there are a number of applications at a higher level. One typical application program is the Corporate Strategic Planning System (CSPS). CSPS uses scenarios and concentrates on key factors and assumptions to generate marketing planning and budget application models for outlining Phillips long-term future. Management no longer has to wait for the data-processing department to generate reports it can produce on its own. In a similar manner, Phillips decision makers determine how to match gas supply and demand with the user-developed Decline Curve Analysis/Forecast System. A hierarchy of data bases containing histories and forecasts for 17,000 wells and detailed, as well as summarized, data base profiles of "typical" well data are used in projecting the decline and production of gas wells. In turn, the Decline Curve Analysis/-Forecast System results are distributed to field personnel via data link from a computer mainframe to their workstations. These workstations are microcomputers and compatible desktop computers—used throughout the decision support system.

Need for Problem Finding in Tactical Marketing Plans. In the future, Phillips plans to make computers and their applications more "human" with futuristic hardware and software that offer voice recognition and expert systems. Essentially, voice recognition systems make it easier for users to interface with computers. In contrast, expert systems "trap" the knowledge and thought processes of one or more experts into a computer so that human reasoning power is available to users when the person or persons are not. Although this represents important computing directions for the company, there is a great need for problem finding at all levels of operations.

The company needs to expand its view of problems (problem finding) by also moving in the direction of a computerized approach. The integration of management science or quantitative models with probing inquiries by middle managers working with corporate planners is what the company needs to do in a tactical marketing DSS operating mode. Important opportunities can be developed by relating them to future problems that can be solved today. Only in this manner will the company have an intelligent solution to tactical marketing plans.

SUMMARY

Tactical planning is the essential linkage between strategic planning and operational planning. It is related not only to middle managers but also to corporate planners as a means of bringing the long term to a shorter time frame. As such, it provides a means of integrating diverse business units into an integrated whole for the coming year. In addition, tactical planning brings the integration of corporate objectives, goals, strategies, and critical success factors down to a very practical level. In essence, managers can be held responsible and accountable for results because the tactical plan is highly measurable.

NOTE

1. "User Friendly DSS Enables Managers, Engineers to Generate Reports," *Information Management*, May 1985, p. 23.

9

Operational Planning and Problem Finding

ISSUES RAISED AND EXPLORED

- How is operational planning different from short-range planning?
- What techniques are helpful in keeping a company at a high productivity level and, at the same time, highly profitable?
- What is the relationship of problem finding to a typical operational plan?
- How can problem finding be of help to the First National Bank of Boston in reaching its stated corporate objectives?

OUTLINE

An Introduction to Operational Planning
Operational Planning versus Short-Range Planning
A Problem-Finding Approach to Operational Planning
Techniques for Improving Operational Performance
   Marketing—PIMS
   Manufacturing—MRP-II
   Finance—ROI

Personnel—HRMS

Development of an Operational Plan Using Problem Finding

Essential Components of an Operational Plan

Integration of Operational Plan with Problem Finding

Operational Planning Example of Problem Finding: First National Bank of Boston

Summary

Strategic planning by top management provides input for tactical planning at the middle management level. In turn, the latter is the basis for operational planning by lower management. Generally, these planning activities are coordinated by corporate planners with the three management levels. Although strategic and tactical planning activities are assisted by decision support systems, operational planning at most small- to large-sized companies is the starting point for computerizing day-to-day, week-to-week, and month-to-month operations. From an overview standpoint, fourth-generation financial modeling languages are used as a way of bringing together operational activities so that actual results can be measured against financial budgets and ratios. It is this viewpoint that underlies operational planning in the chapter where its essential aspects are initially discussed, followed by a problem-finding approach. Techniques for improving operational performance are given, and examples are set forth for integrating operational plans with problem finding.

AN INTRODUCTION TO OPERATIONAL PLANNING

The division of planning into strategic, tactical, and operational phases is convenient for the purposes of exposition. From the point of view of the total planning system, the distinction between phases is not so sharp. However, they differ mostly in the level of detail with which they are specified. At the operational planning level, a production scheduling system, for example, calculates optimal production batching for identical items and to determine the best sequence and run length for each item. This information will then be fed into a production control system that will trigger the appropriate production activities. In turn, the shipment of final goods is supported by a shipping system that updates the inventory records and generates control reports.

OPERATIONAL PLANNING VERSUS
SHORT-RANGE PLANNING

Fundamentally, operating plans allocate tasks to specific facilities in each planning period (week, month, or some other time period) in order to achieve particular objectives. In seasonal businesses, operating plans must reflect seasonal variations in capacities, resolve supplies, product demands, quality requirements, prices, and costs. Operational planning deals in aggregated or average values of variables in the system, such as product demands, equipment capacity, standard costs, and inventory levels.

An example of operational planning is the specification of an oil refinery's quarterly running plan, comprising flow rates, crude oils, and processing conditions required to make the needed amounts of products and blending components. The quarterly running plan establishes ground rules for short-term production planning, such as determining what components will be available with which to blend products according to different formulas.

Short-range planning, like medium-range planning, is an extension of long-range corporate plans. The end result of all short-range planning activities focuses primarily on financial data—that is, flexible (variable) budgets that are developed for stated levels of possible production. To produce detailed balance sheet and income statement data for the coming year, financial data are fed into the corporate computer. The flexible budgeting computer program takes into account the values set forth for the lowest level of expected plant capacity, say 65 percent, and develops corresponding figures for other levels of capacity—70, 75, 80, 85, and 90 percent. Appropriate financial statements are developed and printed for these various levels of capacity. Flexible budgeting data are also written onto the corporate computerized files for comparison with actual figures as they occur month by month.

A PROBLEM-FINDING APPROACH
TO OPERATIONAL PLANNING

Generally, problem finding is found at the higher levels of planning, namely, strategic and tactical. However, if one examines operational planning in some depth, it is not too difficult to determine the need for problem finding. For example, reference can be made to the area of scheduling and dispatching. The objective here is to assign and sequence units of identifiable resources (people, machines, raw materials, and so forth) to manufacture or deliver given quantities of products, consistent with a longer-interval operating plan (such as a quarterly operational plan). At this level, planning deals with specific units and operating rates. Products and facilities must be identified explicitly, and start-up times, sequences of production steps, actual (not average) production rates, unit downtimes, and costs must be treated in detail. Nonlinearities in cost or production functions that are properly ignored or approximated in longer-range planning are critical in scheduling and dispatching.

Based upon these facts surrounding scheduling and dispatching, there are a number of techniques for improving these production control activities. However, the behavioral aspects of how line personnel think and act must be considered. Typically, the approach to manufacturing operations results in "do what you are told and don't ask questions." This one-way directive approach turns many employees off. Hence, they do only what they are told.

In light of this method of managing line personnel, a problem-finding approach is recommended. As a starting point, the production manager calls together a number of production foremen and workers to look at the current situation. An exhaustive look results in a number of problems being uncovered. First, the employees feel that the one-way directive approach to managing results in their ideas being discarded before they can be explored for their worth. In effect, they fail to suggest new ideas even when it is obvious that they should be implemented. Second, as a result of this attitude of management, employees look upon their paycheck as a penalty for work done. Needless to say, this results in a negative attitude toward the company as well as toward their managers. Third, there has been talk of forming a union to overcome the hostility of managers. Instead of helping employees resolve operating problems as well as personal problems, the company disregards the significance of these problems.

Based upon the foregoing behavioral problems, the assembled group felt that all of the problems could be solved more effectively by taking a broad approach. This centers on work redesign such that employees have more power and control over their operations. There is also the need for positive feedback for employees to note their progress. The redesign process looks at the layers of management, each drawing down some authority and responsibility from the one above it. By going up the line and asking "What is there in this job you can let the person below you handle?" employees can undertake certain managerial tasks at the lower levels of manufacturing operations. The net result is that line employees have more control over their operations and feel an integral part of the company.

TECHNIQUES FOR IMPROVING OPERATIONAL PERFORMANCE

Needless to say, there are a number of techniques for improving operational performance in the areas of marketing, manufacturing, finance, and personnel. Due to their importance, the more significant ones are discussed for these areas. Although they focus primarily on problem solving, they can be used as a beginning point to employ problem finding.

Marketing—PIMS

Profit Impact on Marketing Strategies (PIMS) is a computerized approach for planning market strategy that is run by the Strategic Planning Institute. It is a data pool of information on the marketing experiences of its members and encompasses more than 650 product lines.[1] Each member provides PIMS with the most intimate details on matters such as its market share, investment intensity, product quality, and total marketing and R&D expenditures. Through computer simulation, the company can then test its own market strategies against the real experiences of hundreds of comparable companies, including competitors. What it receives are answers to questions such as: What is the normal profit for a business or a product line given its combination of circumstances, and why? If the business continues on its current track, what will its future operating results be? What will happen to short- and long-term performance if certain strategic moves are made? What changes will create the best profit or cash returns?

Essentially, what a member company wants from PIMS is to find out what it will cost to make a particular move and how much better off the business will be afterward. For example, consider return on investment (ROI), which PIMS considers one of the best measures of how a business is doing. The PIMS models can forecast how much ROI for a business line will change because of a strategic move involving more marketing, R&D, capital equipment buildup, or whatever. The models also can forecast what the ROI will be immediately following the move and what it will be several years in the future.

Underlying PIMS Principles. Some new and traditional principles have emerged from PIMS' computer models of the real-life experiences of its corporate members. Among them are: (1) there is a set of operating rules that govern all businesses—thirty-seven factors (including market share, capital intensity, vertical integration, and the like) jointly explain 80 percent of the success or failure of any business; (2) anything more than a minimal research and development program does not make sense for a company with a weak market position; (3) high marketing expenditures for low-quality products can have a devastating effect on profits; (4) high product quality can offset a weak market position; (5) weak companies should not become vertically integrated, whereas strong ones should; and (6) high costs in more than one area, such as capital investment, research and devleopment, or marketing, can ruin any business.

Extrapolating form the PIMS' data base, companies should not automatically compare themselves with competitors in the same industry or business category to find out how well they are doing. According to PIMS, industry breakdowns are not all-important. A better yardstick may be the performance of companies in other industries whose total situation is comparable. A tire company, for example, may have more in common and more to learn from the market strategies of a small appliance manufacturer than from those of another tire company.

Manufacturing—MRP-II

Noted manufacturing systems consultant Oliver Wight (now deceased) spearheaded a movement to raise awareness among manufacturing executives of the need for Material Requirements Planning (MRP). The ABCs of material requirements planning have included: (1) people—the most important element; (2) bills of materials including routings, inventory records, work centers, and the master schedule; and (3) the computer, with an emphasis on software. More recently, MRP has developed into a more significant aspect of priority planning. The original scope of MRP has broadened to encompass all disciplines of a manufacturing company.

MRP has now evolved into "manufacturing resource planning" or MRP-II. In addition to the existing advantages, finance has the ability to monitor costs of company operations on a dynamic basis. Marketing receives valid manufacturing information and, as a result, is able to maintain a valid forecast. Management can now simulate "what ifs" to generate the desired company plan. All this adds up to increased profits. Hence, the original MRP is only a subset of MRP-II.

Oliver Wight believed the most elusive of all goals was making a comprehensive manufacturing MIS (management information system) work. "You can get management support," he commented. "They'll sign the check. But management has to commit itself to running the business more efficiently. In the old days, we thought it [manufacturing system] was a production control system. Today, we know it is a way to run a business."[2] Experience has shown a direct relationship between the level of involvement of the chief executive officer and the eventual success or failure of an implementation plan.

There are many necessary steps on the road to success. These include well-structured bills of materials, sound routings, accurate inventories, and thorough education plans. But none is as important as having the decision-making level of management directing the project. To a large degree, companies accept the concept of a complete manufacturing system without realizing the discipline required to achieve that objective. The person or group initiating the project has the responsibility for bringing management to the required level of understanding.

Finance—ROI

Because return on investment (ROI) is a measure of good, average, or poor performance, management must consider ways of improving it. Divestment of business operations that have a low return, acquisition of investments that have a high return, pruning of low-return product lines, cost reduction and profit improvement, improving asset utilization, and changes in financial structure are constructive ways of increasing a company's return on its investments. An optimal allocation of financial resources that considers these alternatives for increasing ROI is a necessity for reaping a higher return. However, there is a word of caution. If this allocation means raising ROI, it also means balancing long-term commitments and noneconomic constraints, such as social responsibilities. Hence, reduction of commitments seems preferable to taking on a whole series of marginal projects that will reduce the company's ROI in the long run.

Research findings indicate that there is an overall relationship between ROI and investment intensity: the higher the ratio of investment to sales, the lower the return on investment tends to be.[3] This conclusion was drawn from a survey of 57 corporations with 620 diverse businesses. The survey indicated that businesses with high investment intensities are not able to achieve profit margins sufficient to effect the greater amounts of investment they require to sustain a given volume. Another important finding from this study is that market share is a major influence on profitability.[4] ROI rises up steadily as market share increases. On the average, businesses with market shares above 36 percent earned more than three times as much relative to the investment as do businesses with less than 7 percent of their respective markets. Subsequent research strongly suggests the proposition that market share is positively related to the rate of return.[5] Three possible explanations are given: economies of scale, market power, and the quality of management. These factors are quite evident in such major companies as International Business Machines, Gillette, Eastman Kodak, and Xerox. Also, research data indicate that the advantages of a large market share are greatest for businesses selling products that are purchased infrequently by a fragmented customer group.

Personnel—HRMS

Computerized human resource management systems (HRMS) are available to fit the needs of any size corporation. They are relatively easy to install and can pay for themselves in terms of time saved. These systems are staking a vital claim in the structure of the control process. Human resource management systems can be used in various ways to meet internal needs. They can track such information as skills, prior employment, and training courses to aid in career path planning. They can be used for recruiting, training, and educating employees. They can track and administer employee benefits and monitor leaves of absence.

Human resource management systems that are custom-designed can be expensive and often unnecessary. A good packaged system should be flexible enough to provide easy manipulation to meet a corporation's unique needs. It should be easy and economical to install as well as easy to learn and use. Most packaged human resource management systems offer an interface with the payroll system. This expanded data base then allows even more access into employee records. The systems are on-line and records are viewed on a computer terminal. Reports may be formatted and written through the use of a report writer. As corporations continue to grow and employee data record keeping needs continue to increase, they are turning to the computer and packaged HRMS to assist in utilizing their people resources to the best possible advantage.

A summary of the above techniques for improving operational performance is found in Figure 9.1. It should be noted that the techniques are quite useful for strategic and tactical planning. The attendant circumstances will dictate where they should be used; corporate planners may have need of these techniques for different planning purposes.

DEVELOPMENT OF AN OPERATIONAL PLAN USING PROBLEM FINDING

As previously discussed, an operational plan deals in specifics, such as product demands, equipment capacity, standard costs, and inventory levels. Although such activities center on planning, the other side of this "day-to-day operations" coin is *control*. Control is emphasized in order to realize the plan as closely as possible. The main function of control deals with the

Figure 9.1
A summary of typical techniques for improving operational
performance within a corporate planning environment

PIMS (Profit Impact on Marketing Strategies). A computerized approach for planning market strategy that is run by the Strategic Planning Institute. Through computer simulation, the company can test its own market strategies against the real experiences of hundreds of comparable companies, including competitors.

MRP-II (Manufacturing Resource Planning). Centers around manufacturing planning with the addition of monitoring the costs of manufacturing operations. There is need for well-structured bills of materials, sound routings, accurate inventories, and thorough education plans.

ROI (Return on Investment). A measure of good, average, or poor performance which management can use to improve its operational performance. Reseach indicates that the higher ratio of investment to sales, the lower the return on investment tends to be. Also, ROI goes up steadily as market share increases.

HRMS (Human Resource Management System). Useful in tracking such information as skills, prior employment, and training courses to aid in career path planning. It can be used for recruiting, training, and educating employees; it can track and administer employee benefits and monitor leaves of absence.

---

measurement of performance against plan, subsequent adjustment of plans in the light of new conditions, and the feedback of the actual experience to corporate planners if deemed appropriate. It is from this view that an effective operational plan integrates strategic planning and tactical planning with the control function.

Essential Components of an Operational Plan

The essential components of planning are product line and distribution planning, technical and facilities planning, financial planning, and personnel planning. These same planning components are equally applicable to operational planning. The major difference is that they represent the end point of the corporate planning process, thereby providing a basis for controlling daily operational activities. For the first component above, sales quotas are established for salespersons while production standards are used in manufacturing for the second component. For control over the third component, flexible budgets are established. In the last category, personnel performance standards are set as a means for measurement. As indicated previously, the computer is used for comparing budgets and standards, that is, operational plans against actual results.

Typically, problem finding is relegated to financial planning in terms of day-to-day operations in order to improve profitability. However, a more direct route to improved profits has to be through increasing productivity.

Integration of Operational Plan with Problem Finding

An effective operational production plan goes beyond the conventional aspects of the manufacturing facilities by considering the behavioral aspects, or production personnel. More specifically, it employs problem finding to improve productivity and, at the same time, lower manufacturing costs. In effect, it examines new opportunities for work improvement, like work redesign. To integrate operational planning with problem finding, an opportunity-centered approach is employed.

Opportunity-Centered Approach to the Problem-Finding Process. To get started, typically a brainstorming approach (step 1) is used by a work improvement group. After an exhaustive brainstorming session, the group selected an approach that represents the wave of the future in manufacturing (step 2). An essential part of the system is the physical design of the plants themselves. The work environment is quite different from its conventional counterparts.

For starters, there is no time clock, and all employees leave and enter by the same entrance. The conference room is available to all personnel and can be entered from the production side as well as from the general office area. Communication in the plant is open and there are no restrictions on subjects for discussion. Any employee can get in to see the plant manager without having to go through channels. In addition, his office is completely visible through large windows in the corridor that everyone uses to enter the plant; thus, he is not artificially separated from the rest of the plant. The plant manager's office also has the same carpeting and other appointments as the line employees' locker room. The effort to identify all employees as valued participants—not just as superiors and subordinates—starts in the parking lot. Here parking is open and without reserved positions. The most desirable spots go to whomever arrives first. Inside, there is one washroom for men and another for women, one food vending and eating area, and one recreation area.

During the working day, three groups cover the entire range of operations: one processes the products, one packages and ships the products, and one handles supporting office services. Group members rotate among the group's various job positions, and pay rates rise as teammates decide that members are qualified. Members and the group leader decide how the jobs will be rotated. Since there are no traditional departments, group leaders work as equals with group members. Complaints, for example, from customers are given directly to the group members responsible who, in turn, respond by the appropriate means—letter or telephone. Potential applicants for new openings are interviewed by group members, and the decision to hire is made by the group. Although the impression is given that there are just three groups, actually there are a number of subgroups within each area to perform the required operations (step 3).

Although such a system would take a long time to implement successfully, the group estimated that controllable costs (from labor to maintenance) for producing the plant's product volume would fall considerably (say 15 to 20 percent) when compared to the present production facilities. Also, productivity would be up by a comparable amount. Employee motivation and concern for the job would improve considerably. As a result of these dramatic changes, personnel turnover would tend to decrease over time. All in all, problem finding has identified important new opportunities to improve manufacturing operations.

OPERATIONAL PLANNING EXAMPLE OF PROBLEM FINDING: FIRST NATIONAL BANK OF BOSTON

For the First National Bank of Boston, microcomputers are very helpful in analyzing financial statements and assisting in management training.[6] Essentially, the bank is using microcomputers to do financial analysis of customer's financial statements—projections of "what if" situations, analysis, and projection of cash flow, a customer's ability to repay loans, and what might happen under different scenarios. In addition, the bank takes management trainees from business schools and prepares them for positions in its lending management group.

Use of Microcomputers within a DSS Environment for Analyzing Financial Statements. For both areas (analyzing financial statements and assisting in management training), a decision support system approach to microcomputers is used. Previously, terminals linked to a computer mainframe were employed and have been replaced by microcomputers. The microcomputers are being used not only as managerial tools but also as workstations in some situations. The bank's lending area microcomputers are employed to perform financial analysis of customers' financial statements. Using models, written by loan managers, projections of "what if" situations, analysis, and projections of cash flow, a customer's ability to repay loans as well as what might happen under certain scenarios involving interest rate assumptions and loan failure projections are handled by microcomputers. Other examples include the trust department and investment research areas. One user has a multicolumn simulation program that he uses to analyze investments in the oil and gas fields and to show where the best investments lie.

Another major area of microcomputer usage at the First National Bank of Boston is in its Loan Officer Development Program. Here, the bank takes management trainees from business schools and prepares them for positions in its lending management group. In the classroom, the trainees use a microcomputer to access a data base from the credit department and retrieve financial data about the customer they are analyzing. They print the information out on spreadsheets (using Lotus 1-2-3), analyze it, and, upon completion, use the word-processing portion of it to write out their credit report. When trainees graduate, they are literate microcomputer users with a decision support system approach.

Need for Problem Finding in Financial Statement Analysis. For many customers (companies) of the First National Bank of Boston, a review of their financial situation is relatively straightforward since they tend to exceed the criteria needed for a loan. However, there are a sizeable number of companies that just meet the criteria or fall slightly below the established criteria. The question is raised: "Should the loan be granted?" At this junction, a problem-finding approach would be helpful. One approach to problem finding would be the use of *content analysis* of the company's financial statements.[7] Basically, content analysis is used to explore corporate strategy and elements of risk and return. Research reveals that there is a negative correlation of risk and return between companies within industries and a tendency of troubled companies to seek risk.

Another approach to problem finding utilizes the approach of considering whether corporate objectives, goals, and strategies tie in with the company's critical success factors. In other words, is there a good fit among these factors such that the mission of the company is accomplished in a profitable manner? Generally speaking, if there is a good fit, the bank should accept the loan; if there is a poor fit, the loan should be rejected.

For both approaches, the methodology given for the problem-finding process (either the problem-centered approach or the opportunity-centered approach) should be employed. For the first approach, this means that a loan officer would meet with other loan officers to determine the feasibility of making a loan under questionable circumstances. Although problem finding will not guarantee success in each and every case, it should show improvement over other approaches that focus solely on problem solving.

SUMMARY

This chapter has focused on the last planning level—operational planning. At this level, great accent is placed on computerizing operational plans for marketing, manufacturing, finance, and personnel. Even though it may appear that problem finding is not applicable, examples were given to demonstrate how it can benefit a company's day-to-day operations. Problem finding, then, has great potential for improving productivity and, in turn, profits for a typical business organization.

NOTES

1. Paula Smith, "Unique Tool for Marketers: PIMS," *Management Review*, January 1977, pp. 32-34.

2. Wayne L. Rhodes, Jr., "Information Systems in Manufacturing," *Infosystems*, November 1981, p. 41.

3. Sidney Schoeffler, Robert D. Buzzell, and Donald F. Heany, "Impact of Strategic Planning on Profit Performance," *Harvard Business Review*, March-April 1974, p. 143.

4. Ibid., p. 141.

5. Robert D. Buzzell, Bradley T. Gale, and Ralph G. M. Sutten, "Market Share—A Key to Profitability," *Harvard Business Review*, January-February 1975, pp. 97-106.

6. Bill Dooley, "At the Bank of Boston, Doing It Right Means a Personal Computer Center," *Micro Manager*, June 1984, pp. 6-7.

7. Edward J. Bowman, "Content Analysis of Annual Reports for Corporate Strategy and Risk," *Interfaces*, January-February 1984, pp. 61-71.

PART IV

APPLICATION OF PROBLEM FINDING TO SELECTED INDUSTRIES FOR MORE EFFECTIVE CORPORATE PLANNING

10

Application of Problem Finding to the Automobile Industry

ISSUES RAISED AND EXPLORED

- What are the competitive forces and the capacity problems in the U.S. automobile industry?
- What is the linkage of corporate goals to critical success factors for a typical U.S. automobile manufacturer?
- How did the use of short-term CSFs assist Lee Iacocca in saving the Chrysler Corporation from bankruptcy?
- How can the problem-finding process assist the Chrysler Corporation in reaching its stated objectives now and in the future?

OUTLINE

In this final part of the text, problem finding is applied to selected industries. In this chapter reference is made to the automobile industry, while in the final two chapters the airline and computer industries are examined to demonstrate the need for the problem-finding process. This chapter initially centers on an introduction to the U.S. automobile industry which provides a background for the chapter's master case study, the Chrysler Corporation. This is followed by a thorough discussion of the linkage between corporate goals and critical success factors not only for the U.S. automobile industry, but also for the Chrysler Corporation, in particular the company's short-term CSFs. In the last part, the utilization of problem finding at Chrysler is discussed. A conclusion is drawn about the viability of this corporation in the long run.

AN INTRODUCTION TO THE
U.S. AUTOMOBILE INDUSTRY

The automobile industry today is considered to be one of the more mature industries as opposed to high-tech firms of more recent origin. On the home front, the "Big Three"—General Motors, Ford, and Chrysler—dominate the car market although foreign manufacturers (in particular, Japan) have made substantial inroads into the U.S. car market, taking as high as 30 percent of the total market. Based upon U.S. manufacturers' sales performance over the last two decades, General Motors is approximately twice the size of Ford in car and truck sales while Chrysler is about half the size of Ford. Even though these sales figures vary year by year, they approximate the current direction of the U.S. manufacturers. Needless to say, these approximations may change not only due to foreign competition but also due to the aggressiveness of one or two domestic manufacturers.

Competitive Forces in the Automobile Industry

The competititve forces in the industry today versus a few years ago are difficult for the average person to comprehend. Car and truck manufacturers have resorted to a number of incentive programs to maintain their market share. In the past several years, there have been a wide range of factory rebates of some kind plus low interest rate programs. In fact, one manufacturer (American Motors) offered a zero percent rate to stimualte sales. Typically, these incentive programs are offered on slow-moving models and/or when the economy is in the doldrums.

To counteract basic causes of declining sales, some domestic car and truck makers have resorted to new approaches to make their products more competitive. As an example, GM's Pontiac division has turned to producing what one executive calls "expressive cars." For Americans, cars are instruments of self-expression, right up there with sexual fantasies. Pontiac, the only GM division to increase its market share from 1982 to 1985, commissioned a psychologist to study customers' "deepest fantasies about driving." He found that flashy cars made middle-aged women feel younger—hence, the commercial in which a teenager urges mom to cut loose and buy a red Sunbird. For Pontiac, this is something of a return to its modern roots. In the 1960s, under the guidance of John De Lorean, Pontiac built "muscle cars" like the GTO. However, more recently, GM's structure made model differentiation somewhat difficult. It may have been efficient to combine assembly plants and designing and engineering functions in the short run, but the results—look-alike products—were not efficient in the long run.

As another example of how to improve sales as well as meet foreign competition, the Big Three domestic car and truck companies are developing new models for smaller segments of the market—producing as few as 7,000 units instead of the standard Detroit production run of 200,000 or more. Cadillac, for example, is selling the Italian-designed Allante at approximately $50,000 to compete with the Mercedes, BMW, and Jaguar. In doing so, they are changing the way cars are designed and built. They are transforming traditional assembly lines, building in new flexibility so production can be shifted quickly from one model to another. And they are forging international alliances that would have been unthinkable twenty years ago, blurring the distinction between "foreign" and "domestic" cars.

Volumes can be written about the competitive forces of domestic and foreign manufacturers. However, it is safe to say that competition can be expected to be more intensive in the future, thereby signaling a new approach to "getting a handle" on competition. Such an approach is found in problem finding.

Capacity Today versus Tomorrow

In the past, domestic car capacity was fairly well structured; each manufacturer had a number of facilities for assembling cars. This has changed drastically. It is not unusual to read in the press that a certain car assembly plant is being closed for a host of reasons, such as foreign competition and high costs. Because of the balance of payments problem, among other factors, Japanese and other foreign manufacturers have built or are building new car assembly plants in various parts of the United States. As a result, this added capacity of foreign car and truck manufacturers is now causing overcapacity in this country. As even more plants come on-line—foreign as well as domestic—the glut of overcapacity will be even more apparent. The end result is that something must give. Some of the older plants will be closed. The essential message here is that the location of automobile assembly plants will change more rapidly than in the past. In the future, the pace of opening and closing car plants will tend to accelerate.

CHRYSLER CORPORATION: A HISTORICAL PERSPECTIVE

The Chrysler Corporation, founded on May 7, 1921, was incorporated in Delaware on July 6, 1925. It represents a merger of the Maxwell Motor Company and Chalmers Motors Corporation which had previously acquired all of the assets of Dodge Brothers, Inc. Chrysler and its subsidiaries manufacture, assemble, and sell in the United States and Canada its line of Chrylser, Dodge, and Plymouth passenger cars, Dodge trucks, and related automotive parts and accessories. The passenger cars are offered in standard, intermediate, and small-size models. In addition, Chrysler imports and distributes certain small passenger cars and trucks manufactured in Japan by Mitsubishi Motors Corporation. It currently participates in markets outside the United States and Canada, principally through minority investments in automotive companies which are located in such markets. Chrysler has a limited number of subsidiaries and associated companies located outside the United States and Canada that manufacture, assemble, and/or sell Chrysler and Mitsubishi automotive products. Currently, the Chrysler Corporation is the third largest domestic car and truck manufacturer.

Past Problems of Chrysler. Since its incorporation, Chrysler has been known for its engineering. The superiority and world recognition of Chrysler's engineering department was one of the main reasons for its downfall in the past. Chrysler's engineering department operated almost autonomously from the rest of the company. They were designing new cars and features faster than the marketing department could keep up with and faster than the manufacturing department could inform their suppliers for part changes. In addition, once a new car was designed, the engineering department would not work with manufacturing to cure various defects but merely blamed them on poor assembly of the car. This lack of communication was apparent in the introduction of the newly styled Aspen/Volare compacts in 1975. After spending sizable amounts on advertising and dealer promotion, the corporation missed the new car season by at least two months and still was not able to supply the dealers' demand for six to eight months. These time delays were due strictly to a lack of communication between engineering, manufacturing, and the corporation's parts suppliers over specifications and quantities. There were times when an entire day's production would be missed due to parts problems. The situation created not only lost sales but also excessive overhead. Some suppliers became so frustrated that they refused to do business with Chrysler.

The next major problem facing Chrysler was the obsolescence of their manufacturing plants. Management worked its plants and machines right out of business. Whenever there was a downturn in the market, plant improvements were the first expenditure to be cut. Chrysler operated under the theory that labor and energy were always cheaper than purchasing some new piece of equipment. During the oil shortage and labor cost increases in the early 1970s, the shortsightedness of this theory became very apparent. Management was shocked when they learned that the corporation was actually losing money on each car produced at the old Dodge Main Plant, which was one of its first complete assembly plants.

In terms of cost-saving techniques, Chrysler management began tripping over itself. One example was the factory where two- and four-door cars were produced on the same assembly line. Everytime a two door car came down the line, all the peole responsible for the back doors would be without work until another four door came. With cost-saving techniques like this, the corporation knew that it was in trouble. In 1977 (a good sales year), its gross margin per car was only $700 compared to $967 for Ford and $1,465 for General Motors. The corporation knew that as soon as sales started declining it would be in for some real financial problems.

Additionally, the administration of Chrysler lacked sound management techniques. First, it approved the use of the "sales bank" which allowed plants to produce cars without any specific order from a dealer. The car inventories kept building until they ran out of room to store them. Then, the plant would close for three or four weeks until some of the inventory was sold off. This procedure continually provided Chrysler with the largest inventory supply of all the car manufacturers. In addition, management would pressure the sales department toward the end of every quarter to make some deals and sell off some of the inventory before the end of the quarter. It did not take long for the dealers to catch on to this technique; they simply did their heavy buying at the end of each quarter and waited for the good deals. This procedure created serious forecasting problems on a monthly basis since buying was extremely lopsided toward the end of the quarter.

Finally, Chrysler had no real financial controls. It had an accounting department that could tell it how much money they were losing but could not supply management reports needed to analyze the losses and make appropriate corrections. In essence, the corporation was blindly going bankrupt without knowing what to do about it.

On July 13, 1978, the Ford Motor Company announced the firing of Mr. Lee Iacocca. Immediately, Chrysler's chairman of the board and three of its board members independently decided that Chrysler needed Iacocca as its president and chief operating officer if the company was gong to survive. After months of negotiating, a contract was signed and Iacocca joined Chrysler. Even though he was only fifty-four, Iacocca gave up substantial retirement benefits plus approximately $1.5 million in severance pay to go to Chrysler. This by itself was a boost for the morale of Chrysler management and its staff. Iacocca did not realize the current position of Chrysler—the fact that it was truly on the verge of bankruptcy.

The efforts of Iacocca to turn the Chrysler Corporation around have been well documented, including a best-seller by him. Before exploring further the present and future direction of this classic turnaround, the relationship of corporate objectives, goals, strategies, and critical success factors will be discussed. This background serves as a prelude to the utilization of problem finding by Lee Iacocca and his corporate planners and managers.

RELATIONSHIP OF CORPORATE GOALS TO CRITICAL SUCCESS FACTORS IN THE U.S. AUTOMOBILE INDUSTRY

In this text, the model used for implementation of problem finding centered on developing corporate objectives and goals. This was followed by the development of strategies that are linked to the critical success factors. However, to simplify the presentation, corproate goals will be linked directly to CSFs even though there is a strong linkage of the four components to effective problem finding. This is equally true when applying the problem-finding process to the Chrysler Corporation.

Corporate Goals and Critical Success Factors

In the automobile industry, corporate goals and critical success factors for all companies tend to be the same. As illustrated in Figure 10.1, corporate goals (stated amounts) are defined to be high earnings per share, acceptable return on investment, market share growth, and new product success. These corporate goals can undergo changes over time. For example, a corporate goal may be to hire more minority people and women as well as to improve the environment in which the car and truck plants operate.

Figure 10.1
Relationship of corporate goals to critical success factors in the automobile industry

Corporate Goals (Stated Amounts)	Critical Success Factors
High earnings per share	Cost control
Acceptable return on investment	Meet energy standards
Market share growth	Contemporary styling
New product success	Good quality dealer system

Related to these corporate goals are critical success factors, namely, cost control, meeting energy standards, contemporary styling, and good quality dealer system. However, due to fast-changing times, a number of other critical success factors may be necessary to meet established and changing corporate goals. Among these are having quality management from the highest to the lowest level, producing a quality product, and being large enough to effect economies of scale in everyday operations. In regard to the last item, it may be necessary to be a worldwide car and truck company for highly profitable operations. For example, a world-class car, like the Ford Escort, may be necessary to keep development, production, and distribution costs under control. The essential message, then, is that critical success factors—like corporate goals—are not static and should be reviewed by top management and its corporate planners for relevance to the times.

Linkage of Corporate Goals to Short-Term CSFs for the Chrysler Corporation

After Lee Iacocca took over as president and chief operating officer of Chrysler, he initiated a series of programs that were critical to the survival of the corporation—that is, short-term critical success factors. They are given in Figure 10.2. In effect, he set in motion a linkage of the corporation's goals with short-term CSFs as a means of avoiding bankruptcy.

Figure 10.2
Short-term critical success factors identified
for the Chrysler Corporation

1. Strengthen the quality of management
   a. Change the organizational structure
   b. Institute the committee approach
   c. Set up an MBO (management by objectives) program
2. Maintain adequate cash flow for operations
   a. Reduce overhead
   b. Improve working relations with suppliers
   c. Obtain new sources of funds
      1. Stock offerings
      2. Debentures
      3. Banks and insurance companies
3. Improve product quality
4. Achieve government level for fuel economy

First, he had to strengthen the quality of management. He started by completely changing the organizational structure during his third week on the job. He instituted the committee approach for all levels of operations and instituted a management by objectives (MBO) program. He demanded all jobs and functions be cost justified or eliminated. Then he started hiring executives away from the Ford Motor Company and attempted to use Ford management techniques as an example in rebuilding Chrysler's management. He hired Gerald Greenwald to set up accounting systems that would assist management in their daily decisions.

Second, Iacocca needed to improve Chrysler's cash flow. The obvious area to concentrate on first was overhead. He critically reviewed all major operations and executive positions for their necessity and cost justifications. If the areas or individuals were not absolutely required, they were eliminated. In the first two years, he either sold off or closed all unnecessary automotive divisions and all unprofitable nonautomative subsidiaries. During this period, he was able to reduce Chrysler's overhead by approximately $3 billion.

Next, he worked on the corporation's relations with its suppliers. Part of this problem was initially solved when he reorganized the purchasing department under the manufacturing operations. By having the manufacturing department communicate with the supliers, they were able to alleviate some of the initial ordering problems and to solve part defects faster than previously. In addition, Iacocca personally communicated with various suppliers to help explain Chrysler's financial position and to arrange special payment terms. He worked with the manufacturing division to consolidate purchases whenever possible in order to get volume discounts or extended payment terms.

To keep the corporation afloat, he searched for new sources of funds. These evolved around bank and insurance company loans, issuance of debentures, and new stock offerings. Banks and insurance company loans were helpful to Chrysler before going to the U.S. government for loan guarantees and tax credits. In fact, one week before it was publicly announced that Chrysler was on the verge of bankruptcy, Prudential Life Insurance Company lent the company over $40 million on a short-term basis. The issuance of debentures was not a very good source since the company's rating was very low. On the other hand, the issuance of new stock (both common and preferred) through a company- and a union-sponsored employee stock ownership plan (ESOP) and the sale of preferred stock on the open market was quite successful. In both instances, the entire amount of the issuance was sold out.

Third, Iacocca knew that in order to increase the company's

market share and eventually become profitable, the quality of the cars needed to improve drastically. Therefore, during his third week on the job, when he initiated his reorganization plan, part of it involved a new emphasis on a complete quality control program. In prior years, whenever there were employment cutbacks, the quality control department personnel were usually one of the first to go. Under Iacocca's system, quality control groups specialized in different functions of the car (such as doors, windows, electrical systems, and so on) and were given the authority to stop production when certain quality levels were not maintained. These groups also were given the authority to work with suppliers, the engineering department, the assembly division, and whoever else might be involved in order to assure that problems were resolved and not forgotten. In the first two years, Chrysler's reject rate improved by 45 percent and customer satisfaction (per an internal General Motors Report) rated at 78 percent versus 74 percent for General Motors and 72 percent for Ford.

Fourth, the corporation needed to direct more attention toward achieving the government-imposed fuel efficiency level for all cars and trucks. Severe penalties and bad publicity would result from noncompliance. Fortunately for Chrysler, its market for full-size cars was down so badly that they had no problem achieving the level for the first two years.

PROBLEM FINDING AT THE CHRYSLER CORPORATION

Even though Iacocca was successful in merging corporate goals to CSFs in the short term, the success in terms of long-term linkage is yet to be told. In this section, continuing developments of the Chrysler Corporation that are related to problem finding will be examined. Additionally, a brief conclusion will be drawn regarding the viability of this much publicized "Horatio Alger" story of Lee Iacocca.

Essentially, the real survival of Chrysler began in 1979—the fight for the government loan guarantees that eventually bought Iacocca and his team time to reorganize their ailing company. It is an interesting story since corporation executives were pulling together while Congress was divided ideologically on business bailouts. This is especially so since a federal bureaucracy is noted for studying endlessly and accomplishing little. In addition, bankers had given up hope of seeing their money again.

The Chrysler episode is rich enough to offer evidence to support almost any conclusion one wishes. One conclusion is that, on balance, the bailout was not the best response to the corporation's troubles. The saving of Chrysler was a partial failure because not all employees immediately got their jobs back. If saving jobs or avoidance of pain are the goals, there must be a better way than bailing out a corporation. From another viewpoint, the government loan guarantees did not save the corporation, but were a bargaining chip. What really saved Chrysler was sacrifice from labor, creditors, suppliers, and other constituents. The guarantees and those sacrifices were important, but they did not reverse the corporation's decline. Chrysler's managers, given the chance by those guarantees and sacrifices, saved the auto maker. Yet another viewpoint centers on manufacture of the basic K-car. It was stretched out, puffed up, and came up with convertibles, limousines, and minivans. They designed and manufactured a good four-cylinder engine and then fuel-injected it, followed by having it turbo-charged. The net result is that this may be the most versatile small engine in the world. Also, production stressed and hammered in quality. Iacocca convinced Americans that if they could not trust Chrysler, they could trust him. It could not have been done without the bankers and the bureaucrats, and the creditors and the union, but if ever managers deserved credit, this is the case.

Use of Problem Finding to Focus on Competitive Factors. From a pragmatic viewpoint, however, the real story is yet to be told regarding Chrysler's survival in terms of the long run. Fundamentally, this means that the corporation is well advised to get involved in problem finding. For starters, there is the current teaming of General Motors with Toyota to make small cars in the United States. That deal, plus GM's plan to import cars from Japan, may well be the biggest problem clouding Chrysler's future. Chrysler will be looking at bankruptcy or bailouts again. If GM carries out its Japanese strategy, car imports from Japan will climb to 4 million because Chrysler as well as Ford will import them too instead of making them here. The end result is that the United States will be out of the small-car business. This business will not be all in Japan; it will include South Korea. The law of comparative advantage will be extremely hard on Chrysler.

Another problem facing Chrysler as well as GM and Ford is the lack of new technology in small cars Where is the three-cylinder work going on? At this time, it is being performed in Japan—the future of all "bread-and-butter" small cars in this country. When the next oil crunch comes, it is going to go up like a skyrocket. The Japanese are going to have all the three-cylinder engines and all the continuously variable automatic transmissions. What happens if the Japanese have all the economy cars and the United States gets hit with another Arab oil embargo? GM's strategy is to get its small cars from Japan and from the Toyota-GM production deal in California. This means that GM can hold down prices on smaller cars of its Japanese models and make its profits in the middle and upper end of the market it owns, thereby leaving very little to anyone else. Whether Chrysler can operate profitably under these conditions is a difficult question to answer.

Going beyond the problem of small cars, Chrysler could be in a lot of trouble with the labor contract signed with the UAW. It will push labor costs to $25 to $26 an hour in the near future. The corporation's executives seem to have forgotten lessons from the past. Compounding this problem is the fact that the Japanese are not simply better at building small cars. There is a cost advantage that is caused somewhat by the under-valued yen and their tax rebate system. Basically, this difference has nothing to do with labor costs or super-management. Hence, a whole host of problems that are confronting Chrysler in the near and distant future need to be addressed today along with possible solutions to them by employing a problem-finding process. Important opportunities should be identified with these problems currently so that the Chrysler Corporation is assured of its long-term survival.

CONCLUSION

The Chrysler Corporation is a microcosm of everything that is wrong with America. Its problems—increasing union demands, intense competition from foreign car manufacturers, higher fuel costs, more government regulations, and decreasing productivity—are not unique and should be a warning to all companies. Through mismanagement, operational deficiencies, and other important problems, Chrysler put itself on the verge of bankruptcy. Indeed, it had lost its reputation and became synonymous with failure. However, under the strong leadership of Lee Iacocca along with help from the economy, the government, suppliers, and so on, the Chrysler Corporation has been able to regain its place in the automobile industry. However, due to the fast-changing nature of this industry, if the Chrysler Corporation is caught napping on critical problems, it may be facing bankruptcy again. The message, then, is that there is an urgent need to engage in the problem-finding process.

11

Application of Problem Finding to the Airline Industry

ISSUES RAISED AND EXPLORED

- What impact has deregulation had on the U.S. airline industry?
- What is the relationship of corporate goals to critical success factors for a typical U.S. airline?
- Of what benefit are critical success factors to the long-term survival of Delta Air Lines?
- How can the problem-finding process be used to help Delta Air Lines in reaching its present and future corporate objectives?

The structure of this chapter parallels that of the previous chapter, except that the focus is on the airline industry. Due to deregulation, the airlines have become extremely competitive. In order for an airline to grow and prosper, it must become more efficient and plan its moves very carefully. To assist in making the airline more efficient today and tomorrow, there is a great need for problem finding. To place this approach in perspective, the first part of the chapter looks at deregulation and competitive factors in the industry. Next, corporate goals and critical success factors are discussed and related to Delta Air Lines. In turn, this background is helpful to exploring opportunities for Delta in order to maintain its profitable operations. Finally, a conclusion is drawn concerning this well-respected airline.

AN INTRODUCTION TO THE
U.S. AIRLINE INDUSTRY

Like most industries in the United States, the airline industry is dominated by several large carriers. The largest carriers currently include Texas Air (Eastern Airlines, People Express, Continental Airlines, and New York Air), United Airlines, American Airlines, Northwest Airlines, Delta Air Lines, Pan American Airways, and Trans World Airlines. If the past is an indication of the future, this current ordered listing by size of majors can be changed tomorrow by mergers of large carriers with smaller ones. No matter the composition of the airlines, this industry can undergo some very dynamic changes, in particular, the impact of deregulaton on the whole industry. This area plus competitive factors and safety are examined below.

Impact of Deregulation on the Airline Industry

The deregulation of airline routes and fares occurred in 1978. If one examines the facts and figures as the result of deregulation, a considerable amount of new business was generated by cutting fares. As some airline officials say, deregulation saved the industry. It turned it from what would have become a moribund, stagnant industry into a vibrant, growing industry. On the other hand, some say that it was the biggest antilabor bill ever passed. As far as disturbing the status quo for labor, it surely did. But if one looks beyond today and tomorrow, had it not been for that, the industry would have shrunk. And then there would have been far fewer jobs. So what was traded was a few very high-paying jobs for many very good paying jobs. In actuality, both viewpoints have had their day in the current era of deregulation.

Based upon deregulation, the question can be raised: "Will there be an oligopoly for the industry in the long run?" The important thing to remember is that the airline industry under regulation was an even tighter oligopoly. It had more major carriers, but the carriers were not free to compete with one another. Even if as a result of deregulation the industry were to end up with six firms, which will probably not happen, those six are permitted to invade one another's markets. In light of this statement, no one should be concerned about the failure rate among new entrance airlines, particularly because they have been the principal stimulus for intense price competition. But it has been the intensity of competition that has resulted in their disappearance. And no one can deny that the industry is far more competitive now. However, there is a strong likelihood that the deep, intense price competition will abate. Indeed, it is not sustainable because the industry as a whole cannot continue to lose money indefinitely and survive in the long run.

Competitive Factors and Safety in the Airline Industry

The earlier airline system was not regulation in the conventional sense because the Civil Aeronautics Board (CAB) promoted competition. The problem was too much competition, too many flights on too many routes. Thus, the problems of the regulated system were always related to excess capacity. That was demonstrated best in the early 1970s when the airlines suddenly went to jumbo jets and increased capacity so much that the CAB agreed to restrict the number of flights coast to coast. Seldom, if ever, is there a route in the airline industry that justifies more than a normal oligopoly. In that sense, the shakeout to fewer airlines on routes is a good trend.

As a result of competitive factors under deregulation, the average fare paid by passengers is down about 10 percent since 1978. The combination of higher-quality service—takeoffs, landings, and availability—is up about 25 percent over the same period. That is even the case for paying a higher price because the added service offerings more than compensate for the additional price increase. Service increases to small cities and from small cities to hubs have totaled 20 percent. There are more frequent landings and takeoffs in small planes that are more full. Although these represent a step forward for the typical flier, the overall configuring of service is not exactly in keeping with the competitive ideal. But that is true in any industry. One then asks "Is it so far from the ideal that a regulatory structure would work better?" The competitive ideal would be that fares were set only by cost considerations and the distance between two cities, that the number of takeoffs and landings, the quality of the food and service, and the quietness of the airplanes in no way would depend on whether there were two or three or five airlines. Even though that point has not been reached, the service is better given the fact that five airlines are servicing the same two cities.

Finally, advocates of deregulation look only at low fares and frequency of flights; they do not look at the general financial condition of the industry and they choose not to acknowledge the declining safety factor. When one takes into account less money spent on maintenance and the aging of the fleets as the airlines do not have the money to modernize at appropriate rates, one is looking at a system that is for its day technologically inferior to what it was and it is more dangerous. It is absurd to wait for a large number of accidents to admit that there is a safety problem. However, as the shakeout in the industry continues, it will have one benefit. It will tend to stabilize the structure of the industry and restrict competition somewhat.

DELTA AIR LINES: A HISTORICAL PERSPECTIVE

As in the past, Delta Air Lines is today one of the more profitable airline carriers. This has been caused in part by a unique relationship among its employees, sometimes referred to as "the Delta family." Talk of the family concept at Delta is not just public relations. This is a company where three flight attendants started a campaign in 1982 that resulted in employees voluntarily purchasing a $30 million Boeing 767 after Delta had an unprofitable quarter. If a sick employee has used up his or her paid leave, Delta allows other employees to work for the individual so that his or her paycheck is not lost.

In an industry where major carriers have been and are scrambling to expand their route systems, Delta has been slow. The frenzy of mergers and acquisitions in the industry are aimed at achieving the economies of scale believed necessary for survival in the current low-fare environment. And more than a few carriers are threatening inroads into Delta's southeastern U.S. stronghold.

To a large degree, Delta's holding pattern is self-imposed. The carrier has long had a policy of expanding internally rather than through acquisitions, such as the expansion of its minor hub in Cincinnati into a major one. After years of carefully avoiding union organizing—the pilots are the only large group of unionized Delta employees—it is loathe to acquire another heavily unionized carrier. At the same time, however, Delta is constrained from adding a rash of new flights and hiring new pilots at one of the highest pay scales in the industry. The average compensation for all Delta employees in 1985, including benefits, was $49,852, compared with the major airlines average of $43,819. Delta finds it difficult to make any expansion moves until it resolves its pilot pay rates; that is, Delta wants to get their contract squared away.

With its major competitors picking up routes amid the recent acquisitions and with American Airlines beginning to challenge Delta's largely eastern routes, Delta can little afford to stand still. American has developed hubs in Raleigh/Durham, North Carolina, and Nashville, Tennessee. As one analyst put it, "You either get bigger or you get smaller." In light of the dilemmas facing it, Delta decided to acquire Los Angeles–based Western Airlines for $860 million in 1986, allaying speculation that Delta was too cautious for its own good. Delta stood pat while rivals were getting bigger in the recent airline merger mania, but Mr. Garrett—the company's chairman and chief executive officer—said the company was just waiting for the "right" transaction. He summed up his merger philosophy this way: "For a merger to be worthwhile, two plus two has to equal seven." Garrett—whose reputaiton is that of a thorough, cautious planner who worked his way up at Delta as an operations expert—said Delta began studying Western more than two years ago. The two airlines began discussing a joint marketing agreement in the winter of 1985. The more they looked at it, the more they realized how both systems fit together logically. American Airlines is most likely to feel the fallout from the merger. All Western employees are guaranteed jobs but Delta still must work out how to merge Western's unionized and lower-paid employees into its own mostly nonunion and higher-paid work force.

RELATIONSHIP OF CORPORATE GOALS TO CRITICAL SUCCESS FACTORS IN THE U.S. AIRLINE INDUSTRY

As in most industries, there are a number of corporate goals that can be related to specific critical success factors for the U.S. airline industry. Also, there is need to examine the critical success factors for Delta Air Lines. Due to their importance, both areas are covered below.

Corporate Goals and Critical Success Factors

Generally speaking, corporate goals tend to be the same for all types of activities. However, their critical success factors differ by the type of airline, whether it be low-cost, no frills (like People Express) or full service (like Delta) carriers. In Figure 11.1, corporate goals are given as high earnings per share, acceptable return on investment, market share growth, and high-quality service. Due to deregulation, these basic goals could change to include having a fuel-efficient fleet, if fuel prices again become a significant factor in profitability, as well as having a low debt-equity ratio.

In light of typical current corporate goals in the industry, a number of critical success factors can be developed which are shown in Figure 11.1. They include high-revenue passenger yield, effective cost control, use of the hub concept, and the reputation as a safe and dependable carrier. As times change, so will these important factors. Use of fuel-efficient propfan engines for reducing operating costs and the elements of high union salaries could be the most critical factors facing an airline for survival. Thus, CSFs for this industry tend to change more as a result of deregulation.

Figure 11.1
Relationship of corporate goals to critical success factors in the airline industry

Corporate Goals (Stated Amounts)	Critical Success Factors
High earnings per share	High-revenue passenger yield
Acceptable return on investment	Effective cost control
Market share growth	Reputation as a safe and dependable carrier
High-quality service	Use of the hub concept

Linkage of Corporate Goals to CSFs for Delta Air Lines

In reference to Delta Air Lines, the merger of Western has created one of the largest scheduled air carriers. This merger represents a culmination of two years of work. Delta was the nation's sixth-largest airline in terms of revenue passenger miles, while Western ranked ninth. When they combine, the new entity will fly more than 40 billion revenue passenger miles a year, putting it one or two positions ahead of its past ranking.

In view of this merger, Delta needs to review its corporate goals as they relate to its critical success factors. Although its corporate goals may be still relevant for the times, a revised list of long-term CSFs is found in Figure 11.2. The first four items in the list—taken from Figure 11.1—are about the same, except for the second item where there is need for a fuel-efficient fleet. Fundamentally, these critical factors are related to keeping Delta one of the most profitable airlines and maintaining its reputation as the most professional airline among travelers.

Figure 11.2
Revised listing of critical success factors identified for Delta Air Lines in the long run

1. High-revenue passenger yield per mile flown
2. Effective cost control, including a low-cost, fuel-efficient fleet of planes
3. Reputation as a safe and dependable carrier
4. Use of the hub concept in larger cities
5. Enhancement of the "family" concept
6. A flexible route structure with a comprehensive feeder system
7. Development of strategies to aid sales during seasonal lows
8. Integration of domestic growth with international system growth

To maintain its enviable position in the airline industry and, at the same time, reach corporate goals effectively, it must consider new CSFs that are complementary to the present ones. Inasmuch as the Delta system centers on the eastern, midwestern, and southern sections of the country while Western centers on the western part, there is need for a flexible route structure such that planes can be taken off certain routes and used to meet seasonal needs in various parts of the country. For example, in the winter, the south is a very desirable destination for easteners and midwesterners. The same cannot be said for summer when traffic to the south slows. An integral part of this flexible route structure is a comprehensive feeder system. Going beyond this country's borders, there is need for integrating the domestic market with the international one where it logically fits together. In effect, the domestic market feeds the international market. All in all, the critical factors that determine success or failure need to be addressed by management today before competition gets the upper hand.

PROBLEM FINDING AT DELTA AIR LINES

In the preceding discussion, Delta and its employees had what they regarded as a family relationship. But discount fare wars and deregulation have taken their toll on Delta's generosity and are putting some strain on the family. Delta needs wage and work-rule concessions from its employees to compete in a deregulated industry. Lower wages from its employees are needed to operate profitably, and the integration problem caused by the Western merger must be resolved. At the same time, it must explore today what problems and opportunities in the future will make or break the airline.

As a starting point for identifying new opportunities, reference can be made to the use of the hub concept in larger cities. Delta's hubs have been expanded by the merger of Western. (This is the fourth CSF in Figure 11.2.) The relationship of routes is best demonstrated by looking at a map overlaid with both of their routes. Delta's routes blanket most of the eastern and southeastern United States with major hubs in Atlanta, Dallas/Fort Worth, and Cincinnati; Western's routes saturate the United States west of the Rocky Mountains with hubs at Salt Lake City and Los Angeles. As more of a national carrier, Delta will find it much easier to keep passengers who previously had to switch to another airline to complete their journey. Likewise, with this expanded route system the combined airline can now think in terms of expanding its international markets (eighth factor). The same rationale about switching to another carrier also applies here.

Because Western has been a union shop and Delta basically has not been, the family concept (fifth factor) provides an underlying framework for merging the two "corporate cultures." That is, Delta stands for something in the eyes of its employees and, in many respects, is a replacement for a union shop. If Western employees see and like this family atmosphere, the problems that have been caused by the merger will tend to be minimized over time. The implementation of the family concept is critical since Delta plans to phase out the identity of Western, an airline that traces its history back farther than any other U.S. carrier to the first scheduled flight of Western Air Express in 1926.

Regarding strategies to aid sales during seasonal lows (seventh factor), Delta's corporate planners should seek new opportunities for expanding untapped markets. For example, Delta could institute corporate discounts to help fill empty seats during off-season periods. Under such a system, major corporations would contract with one or more carriers for substantial discounts in return for all of their business travel needs. With a stronger national route system, Delta could benefit greatly from such a move.

In a similar manner, Delta needs to explore opportunities for expanding its sales during the winter travel season. This may mean working its employees longer hours where permitted by law and leasing planes for short periods of time. This opportunity can be expanded to developing Delta charters that specialize in weekend departures from large population centers to fun and vacation spots in this country and abroad. In this manner, the airline is catering not only to business people throughout the week but also to vacationers who may like to take weekend trips. The low-cost air fares now make the weekend vacations possible for a large segment of society.

Additionally, opportunities abound in more effective cost control (second factor). Cost reduction can take place on the ground as well as in the air. For example, better use of television monitors at each gate would eliminate the need for personnel to direct deplaning passengers. Too often, these personnel waste a large part of their day waiting for arrivals. In the air, Delta needs to be on the forefront of new technology, including use of the propfan engine which is capable of effecting significant fuel savings over the conventional jet engine. This cost-saving approach is needed especially with anticipated periods of high fuel prices. Failure to be aggressive in this area may result in trying to compete with airlines that have made a major commitment in this new direction of cost savings.

The foregoing opportunities have, by no means, exhausted the possibilities for the combined airline. The opportunity-centered approach can be used to great advantage. Similarly, the problem-centered approach can be utilized to resolve problems today that are seen lurking in the future. In essence, the problem-finding process can be extremely helpful to Delta's corporate planners to improve performance at all levels and enhance the family concept of the merged airline.

CONCLUSION

When Congress deregulated the airline industry, it unleashed the powerful forces of competition into a field that had been tightly controlled. For the first time, travelers have real choices. They can pick an American or a United, a Continental or a Delta. The competition has produced a certain amount of confusion, and the best fares are not always easy to locate quickly. But passengers today have a better chance than ever of flying where they want to go, when they want to go, and at a price they want to pay. For Delta to continue its profitable operations, it must understand these important facts and integrate them into its corporate plans. This means making use of the problem-finding process to ensure that corporate plans are as optimal as possible for the short run to the long run. Overall, corporate plans that utilize problem finding must recognize the importance of placing the customer first, followed by building a family concept around the idea that the "customer is king."

12

Application of Problem Finding to the Computer Industry

ISSUES RAISED AND EXPLORED

- What impact has foreign competition had on the U.S. computer industry?
- What is the relationship of corporate goals to critical success factors for a typical computer firm?
- How can critical success factors be useful to the long-term survival of the Digital Equipment Corporation?
- In what ways can the problem-finding process be employed to assist the Digital Equipment Corporation in reaching its present and future corporate objectives?

In this last application of problem finding, the computer industry is examined. For years, the industry has averaged approximately 20 percent annual growth. However, its recent slowdown has prompted some debate about the outlook, but it is widely believed that the pace of expansion will again pick up. Faith in the basic laws of "computernomics" prevails. Each year, engineers cram more circuits on the same piece of silicon, enabling a dollar's worth of computer to do more work. Meanwhile, customers' hunger for power grows as they enter mountains of information into their machines and use them for a wider range of applications. Computer manufacturers share this view. To place this whole industry into perspective, the accent is on competition—the first matter for discussion in the chapter. This is followed by relating corporate goals to critical success factors for a typical company in this industry. Corporate goals are linked to CSFs for the Digital Equipment Corporation (DEC), and problem finding in terms of market opportunities is explored for it.

AN INTRODUCTION TO THE
U.S. COMPUTER INDUSTRY

In this growth industry, the contrast between big and small is staggering. Basically, the industry is one that has been dominated by one company, IBM, sometimes called "Big Blue." The other large computer manufacturers are normally referred to as the others—Unisys (formerly Burroughs and Sperry Univac), Control Data, DEC, Honeywell, and NCR. However, the firm that is giving IBM a run for its money is the Digital Equipment Corporation. Today, the name of the computer game is not to meet IBM head-on across the board but to specialize in areas that are not dominated by IBM.

Competitive Forces in the Computer Industry

Over the past several years, the International Business Machines Corporation collected 40 percent of the computer industry's revenue and 70 percent of its profit. Already the world's most profitable industrial company, it doubled in size in the past six years and could double again in the early 1990s. In a few words, IBM towers over its competitors, the object of imitation, envy, and accusations that it is just too powerful for the world's good. Downturns do not shake IBM's faith in the industry's future. It simply weather such storms better than others, continuing to invest billions of dollars into R&D, new factories, products, and office buildings.

IBM forges ahead, in part, because it thinks technology will play an extremely important part of its strengths in the years ahead. Upstarts will always engineer computers that are a little faster and cheaper than IBM's and write programs that are a little more brilliant. These entrepreneurs usually are billed as the heroes of high technology, while big business is unresponsive and inept. Despite prevailing wisdom, size can confer considerable advantages because some industrial processes typically do not work without teamwork on a vast scale. Although great technological advances often begin with a lone scientist's discovery, most people do not benefit until that discovery is refined, tested, and incorporated into low-cost, mass-produced goods shipped to the far corners of the world.

Although IBM has been mass producing business equipment for nearly a century, its early machines were more primitive and less pervasive than the computers, software, typewriters, telephones, and robots that IBM sells today. The company has rarely pioneered, but promising new segments do not long escape its attention. That was true for computer mainframes in the 1950s when IBM grabbed Sperry Univac's initial lead, and for personal computers in the 1980s when IBM surpassed Apple and the rest of the market to earn the largest share. However, the challenge currently is implementation, that is, building global computer networks that work as reliably and as easily as the telephone system does today. It is something small organizations just cannot do alone, and IBM is already facing giant new competitors like Ameican Telephone & Telegraph Company and General Motors Corporation.

Another important challenge to IBM has been coming from DEC. Digital's computers have the capacity to talk to each other seamlessly, a capability IBM did not have until just recently. Urged on by customers, the computer industry has embarked on a new era of "connectivity." But because of a strategic move almost two decades ago, Big Blue is saddled with a mishmash of machines that are not on speaking terms with each other. The lack of links hurts IBM most in the minicomputer market. There IBM, legendary for its marketing prowess, is taking a drubbing from Digital Equipment. Digital, which is less than one-sixth IBM's size, is moving beyond its traditional technical customers into classic IBM markets.

Additionally, IBM has been losing significant sales to Digital as customers tire of IBM's confusing array of five incompatible midsize families with five separate software systems. However, the debut of its latest line—the so-called 9370 family—borrows Digital's one-software-fits-all approach by using several hundred thousand programs that IBM mainframe customers already use on some 27,000 machines. The new line is the biggest IBM move yet to counter Digital's inroads. For the first time, its new family will work on a networking approach known as Ethernet, pushed heavily by Digital. And IBM officials took the rare step of directly comparing their new machines with Digital products, despite company policy against specifically discussing rivals, and said the lowest-priced IBM model is much more powerful than a comparable Digital machine.

As can be seen from the foregoing, the competition between IBM and DEC is becoming more intense than in the past. The competition will increase in years to come. In addition, it will be related to foreign competition.

Foreign Impact on the Computer Industry

IBM's overwhelming dominance of the personal computer market is being sharply eroded by clones—less complex, often non-brand name machines produced at low cost in the Far East. In the short term, IBM is trying to reduce their threat by bolstering relations with dealers. At the same time, it intends to introduce a new personal computer system that will sell for under $1,500, possibly $1,295—a price that would make it more competitive with the clones. In the longer run, IBM is expected to introduce personal computers that contain more proprietary hardware and software. The new computers are expected to run programs written for the operating system (MS-DOS) that is now used on the current generation of IBM-compatible computers.

From a diffrent perspective, IBM's market share in Japan has slipped in recent years. IBM, once number one, then number two to Fujitsu, Ltd., fell to third place in 1984, behind NEC Corporation. Given Japan's strength in technology and manufacturing and nationalistic attitudes, competing in East Asia is exceedingly difficult. Checking the Japanese in their back yard is critical if only to fend off the Japanese in the West. In product after product, IBM is striving to cut manufacturing costs to the bone to fend off Japanese competitors. It is a challenge U.S. companies in some other industries have lost.

DIGITAL EQUIPMENT CORPORATION: A HISTORICAL PERSPECTIVE

Digital Equipment Corporation is the largest minicomputer manufacturer in the world. In 1957, it was founded by Kenneth H. Olsen and two partners with an initial capital of $70,000. Prior to this period, computers were large machines that were environmentally controlled. Only large companies could afford them and only relatively few professionals were capable of operating them or understanding them. Like Henry Ford and George Eastman, who took expensive, esoteric products and produced them for a mass market, Olsen believed that computers could serve a wide array of business functions if they were designed for ease of use. In essence, this is what he did in a very short time.

Starting with the first minicomputer, it took three years for DEC to assemble. Five years later, the company introduced the PDP-8—the computer that created the minicomputer industry and the whole concept of *distributed data processing* (DDP).

Essentially, DDP makes use of many small computers dispersed throughout an organization which, in turn, are connected to one or more large computer mainframes. Over the years, DEC's product line proliferated to include several different types of processors designed for many different markets. DEC has grown to become a multibillion-dollar company operating in forty countries on five continents. Digital facilities around the world include 28 major manufacturing plants, 198 sales offices, 26 training centers, 400 field sales offices, and administrative and support operations worldwide.

DEC's broad line of computers includes microcomputers, minicomputers, and computer mainframes. System prices range from less than $1,000 to over $1 million. DEC also produces a wide variety of peripheral equipment, including magnetic storage devices, cathode ray tube display systems, terminals, and line printers. Selected peripheral equipment of other manufacturers is purchased by DEC for use with its own computer systems. To serve customers effectively and efficiently, DEC is structured around a number of operating groups dedicated to specific markets.

The corporation is one of the most decentralized major companies in the United States. Most of the U.S. corporate world is organized from the top down. But Olsen consciously designed DEC for ideas to flow from the bottom up. In the minicomputer field, changes occur fast. The average product life is around two years and, if innovations are to be made from the top, the decisions probably will be inappropriate by the time they are carried out. DEC uses a "matrix" organization that is organized by both functions and product lines at the same time. Each market segment has a manager where the individual has very broad responsibilities. The manager not only serves a particular set of customers but also develops new products and is charged with profit and loss responsibility.

The market segment managers call on the services of engineering, production, and sales groups. The people who serve the market segments report both to the heads of their functional group and to the market segment manager. This matrix organization structure is designed to create an entrepreneurial spirit. Each market segment acts like a smaller company. The responsibility for new product development is pushed down to the level of managers who are close to the market. This helps stimulate creative engineering that sells. In turn, market segment managers are judged chiefly on how happy they make customers. The salespersons are salaried. Their performance is also measured by customer satisfaction (that is, determined through an annual survey). The executives spend a great deal of their time in face-to-face talks and in travel. Thus, DEC is a "market-driven organization" versus a "product-line company."

RELATIONSHIP OF CORPORATE GOALS TO CRITICAL SUCCESS FACTORS IN THE U.S. COMPUTER INDUSTRY

To understand better the relationship of corporate goals to critical success factors, reference can be made to one of the first presidents of IBM. The legend of Thomas J. Watson, Sr., who came to manage the company in 1914, looms large. His philosophy can be found in a series of 1962 lectures that were published under the title "A Business and Its Beliefs." Preachers know good sermons make at most three points, and the Watson philosophy was simple, too. One, give the *best service* of any company in the world. Two, strive for *superior performance*. Three—the one IBMers think is most important—*respect the individual*. The degree to which the third belief holds may be IBM's most remarkable asset. It is singled out by nearly everybody at the company. Even those who depart praise the way IBM treats people and the way it makes them feel they belong. Underlying corporate goals and critical success factors explored below is this important contribution by Mr. Watson.

Corporate Goals and Critical Success Factors

Corporate goals found in the computer industry are not too much different from those in other industries. As shown in Figure 12.1, they include high earnings per share, acceptable return on investment, maintaining market share growth, and innovative products. Due to changing times, they may include such items as rewarding company personnel for superior performance and emphasizing a humanistic approach to managing people.

Figure 12.1
Relationship of corporate goals to critical success factors in the computer industry

Corporate Goals (Stated Amounts)	Critical Success Factors
High earnings per share	Technological leadership
Acceptable return on investment	Effective cost control
Maintaining market share	Good customer service
Innovative products	Product compatibility

There are a number of critical success factors that are linked to goals. Four important CSFs are found in Figure 12.1. They are technological leadership, effective cost control, good customer service, and product compatibility. This listing will undoubtedly be supplemented by other ones. Not only will they center on customers in terms of making computers more "user friendly," but they will be related to the individual workers such that the individual feels that his or her job is worth going to every day. From either viewpoint, the underlying framework is to improve productivity, making the user more productive or assisting the employee such that the job is easier.

Linkage of Corporate Goals to CSFs at the Digital Equipment Corporation

The linkage of corporate goals to CSFs is paramount. Essentially, DEC's corporate goals are analogous to those in Figure 12.1. As they are essentially self-explanatory, the focus here will be on CSFs.

In terms of technological leadership (first critical success factor in Figure 12.1), it is absolutely necessary for DEC to innovate continuously and offer new products such that they become the new standards in business. Also, development should center on small, inexpensive systems while offering the broadest range of computer hardware, software, and related services in the industry. Diversity and the high quality of DEC's products have kept it number one in the highly competitive minicomputer market.

A most important CSF is effective cost control (second factor). As discussed previously in the chapter, there are a number of foreign clones that can accomplish the same computing tasks at a much lower cost. Although the quality is somewhat lower than at DEC, quality will be on the same level very shortly. At this point, cost becomes the important ingredient in buying from DEC or from abroad. Thus, DEC must automate its plants so that costs are as low as possible. Otherwise, the business which they have worked so hard to cultivate over the years may go elsewhere to save money.

In terms of customer service (third factor), there is need to give prompt service to customers. One way for DEC's customers to reduce costs and improve productivity is having their computers up and running at all times as opposed to waiting for service. DEC has a very large field service operation with 480 locations around the world and over 20,000 customer service employees. They have a mobile van repair service for quick response to on-site terminal service calls, very innovative computer-aided telephone maintenance systems, and new "carry-in" service centers for terminal customers. They have set up depot maintenance systems and are concentrating on efforts to lower the cost of ownership of their computers by the way in which they supply customer services.

To avoid one of IBM's major problems currently, DEC must stress product compatibility (fourth factor). It is essential that the compatibility be designed to maximize the computer's ability to meet current user needs and to permit the addition of more computers as the user's needs grow in the future. This requirement goes beyond just hardware. Creating software compatibility is necessary so that DEC's software can be used from system to system and across generations of computers. This will help protect the user's investment. DEC devotes a great deal of research and development to create compatibilty of its hardware and software.

PROBLEM FINDING AT THE DIGITAL EQUIPMENT CORPORATION

Employing these CSFs today has helped DEC to make important inroads into IBM's customer base. Because some IBM customers have become impatient, they are trying Digital's VAX minicomputer series which uses the same software for the whole line—from desktop machines to powerful computer mainframes. As one big IBM customer said: "My business problems are today. Why should I wait for IBM?" In addition, DEC has beat IBM on the whole concept of connectivity, a networking approach that ties computers in various locations together. Although DEC has the upper hand at this point for many current CSFs, what Big Blue will introduce tomorrow can have a devastating impact on DEC. To assist from getting caught, the corporation should engage in problem finding as if its survival depended on it. More to the point, it should seize new opportunities to beat or at least meet competition.

In order to increase sales, the corporation needs to explore new market opportunities. DEC should explore training its sales personnel in selling executive and office work systems. The group that has been marketing word-processing products to key accounts should now expand their sales potential to stand-alone management work stations that are needed within a DSS operating mode and word-processing units that go beyond just word processing. The new group should also act as a liaison between the office product specialist in each marketing group and the engineering group dedicated to office product development. Top management should give guidelines to marketing managers regarding product margins. Salespeople should be given incentives to improve performance.

The corporation should take advantage of its large customer base in minicomputers. Existing customers will find it easier to justify the cost of new executive and office work systems if they are partially leveraged by investment in DEC's products. Salespeople should stress DEC's compatibility feature. DEC should also take advantage of its strength as a satellite processor vendor. (Satellite processing systems act as host computer terminals and work stations while communicating through local networks to large, corporate data-processing centers, which usually consist of IBM computer mainframes.)

Building upon the above, the company should explore added market opportunities in the area of education. DEC has sold or lent computers to colleges and universities, starting in 1960. As a result, a whole generation of scientists and business people learned about computers with DEC equipment. Many of them are DEC customers now. However, not all people go on for a degree. Thus, DEC should consider making a strong bid for microcomputers and minicomputers now being installed in high schools. Just as college graduates have helped DEC emerge as a large equipment manufacturer, the same approach can be used on high school students.

Opportunities for improvement go beyond marketing the products to what products should be marketed. The corporation needs to find out what the customer wants in order to be more market driven versus product driven. This may mean working the diversity of new products by offering standard packages of equipment, especially for commercial users. In addition, Digital should identify and eliminate product overlaps before new systems are introduced.

Essentially, the foregoing opportunities have centered on marketing. However, similar opportunities can be identified for some of the company's other problems. Digital's problems are in the areas of manufacturing, finance, and personnel. In a similar manner, there is need to find organizational problems that have an impact on the company. Periodically, it is beneficial to reorganize the organizational structure in order to keep from lagging behind its corporate size and, at the same time, to adapt to the rapidly changing external environment.

CONCLUSION

To some extent, the Digital Equipment Corporation is fortunate in being a leader in an industry of growing importance to the world's economy. Powerhouses in other industries once played similar roles, only to stumble before foreign competitors, demanding unions, bureaucratic management, or economic forces beyond their control. Digital shows no signs of faltering at this point in time but rather moves with an agility that belies its size. In the past several years, DEC has put itself through significant changes to meet IBM head on in many fronts. Managing DEC—keeping it growing, profitable, and abreast of technology—is a large balancing act that can be better accomplished through the employment of the problem-finding process.

Bibliography

Basadur, M., Graen, G. B., and Green, S. G. "Training in Creative Problem Solving: Effects on Ideation and Problem Finding and Solving in an Industrial Research Organization." *Organizational Behavior and Human Performance*, Vol. 30, 1982.

Cowan, D. A. "Developing a Process Model of Problem Recognition." *Academy of Management Review*, Vol. 11, No. 4, 1986.

Davis, K. R. "The Process of Problem Finding: A Production-Marketing Example." *Interfaces*, Vol. 8, NOP. 1, November 1977.

Getzels, J. W. "Problem Finding and the Inventiveness of Solutions." *Journal of Creative Behavior*, Vol. 1, 1975.

_____. "Problem Finding." The 343rd Convocation Address, University of Chicago, *University of Chicago Record*, Vol. VII, No. 9, November 21, 1973.

Graham, R. J. "Problem and Opportunity Identification in Management Science." *Interfaces*, Vol. 6, No. 4, August 1976.

Isenberg, D. J. "Thinking and Managing: A Verbal Protocol Analysis of Managerial Problem Solving." *Academy of Management Journal*, Decembner 1986.

Kilmann, R. H., and Mitroff, I. I. "Problem Defining and the Consulting Intervention Process." *California Management Review*, Spring 1979.

Lasden, M. "Computer-Aided Decision Making." *Computer Decisions*, November 1982.

_____. "Enriching the Decision-Making Process." *Computer Decisions*, November 1983.

Leavitt, H. J. "Beyond the Analytic Manager." *California Management Review*, Vol. XVII, No. 3, Spring 1975.

_____. "Beyond the Analytic Manager: Part II." *California Management Review*, Vol. XVII, No. 4, Summer 1975.

Martin, A. P. *Think Proactive: New Insights into Decision Making.* New York: The Professional Development Institute, 1984.

Millar, V. E. "Decision-Oriented Information." *Datamation*, January 1984.

Oxenfeldt, A. R., Miller, D. W., and Dickinson, R. A. *A Basic Approach to Executive Decision Making.* New York: AMACOM, 1978.

Pascarella, P. "The New Science of Management." *Industry Week*, January 6, 1986.

Pounds, W. F. "The Process of Problem Finding." *Industrial Management Review*, September 1971.

Quintelier, G.L.M. "A Technique for Problem Finding and Market Introduction." *Rersearch Management*, September 1978.

Raitt, R. A. "Must We Revolutionize Our Methodology?" *Interfaces*, February 1984.

Sanderson, M. "Successful Problem Finding." *Journal of Systems Management*, October 1974.

Sowell, T. *Knowledge and Decisions.* New York: Basic Books, 1980.

Susman, G. I. "Planned Change: Prospects for the 1980s." *Management Science*, February 1981.

Taylor, R. N. "Nature of Problem Ill-Structuredness: Implications for Problem Formulation and Solution." *Decision Sciences*, Vol. 5, 1974.

Thierauf, R. J. *Effective Management Information Systems*, 2d ed. Columbus, Ohio: Charles E. Merrill, 1987.

_____. *User-Oriented Decision Support Systems—Accent on Problem Finding.* Englewood Cliffs, N.J.: Prentice-Hall, 1988.

Index

About the Author

ROBERT J. THIERAUF is Professor of Information and Decision Sciences at Xavier University, and served as chairman of the Department of Management for 13 years. He has also worked in industry performing audits and consulting. He is the author of 18 books, many of which have been translated into other languages including Spanish, German, Russian, and Japanese. He is a member of the Academy of Management, the American Institute of Certified Public Accountants, The Institute of Management Science, the Decision Sciences Institute, and the Association for Computing Machinery.